# SIMPSONS COMICS

# SIMPSORAMA

HarperPerennial

*A Division of* HarperCollins*Publishers*

To the loving memory of Snowball I:
9 lives never went so fast.

SIMPS-O-RAMA Copyright ©1995 & 1996 by
Bongo Entertainment, Inc. All rights reserved.
No part of this book may be used or reproduced in any manner whatsoever
without written permission except in the case of brief quotations
embodied in critical articles and reviews. For information address:
HarperCollins Publishers, Inc.
10 East 53rd Street, New York, NY 10022
1999 Avenue of the Stars, Los Angeles, CA 90067

HarperCollins books may be purchased for educational, business,
or sales promotional use. For information, please write:
Special Markets Department, HarperCollins Publishers, Inc.
10 East 53rd Street, New York, NY 10022

FIRST EDITION
ISBN 0-06-095199-0

96 97 98 99 00 RRD 10 9 8 7 6 5 4 3 2 1

Publisher: MATT GROENING
Managing Editor: JASON GRODE
Art Director/Editor: BILL MORRISON
Book Design: MARILYN FRANDSEN
Legal Guardian: SUSAN GRODE
Contributing Artists:
BILL MORRISON, TIM BAVINGTON, PHIL ORTIZ, LUIS ESCOBAR,
STEPHANIE GLADDEN, TIM HARKINS, NATHAN KANE, ERIC MOXCEY,
DAVID MOWRY, JEANNINE CROWELL, SCOTT SHAW!,
CHRIS UNGAR, SHAUN CASHMAN, CHRIS ROMAN
Contributing Writers:
BILL MORRISON, GARY GLASBERG, ROB HAMMERSLEY,
TODD J. GREENWALD, SCOTT M. GIMPLE, BARRY DUTTER,
JON AIBEL, GLENN BERGER, JEFF ROSENTHAL, SCOTT SHAW!

PRINTED IN CANADA

# CONTENTS

## SIMPSONS #11

7   FALLEN FLANDERS

30   THE KWIK-E AND THE DEAD!

## SIMPSONS #12

38   SURVIVAL OF THE FATTEST!

60   SPARE THE ROD,
SPOIL THE GRUNT!

## SIMPSONS #13

69   GIVE ME MERCHANDISING
OR GIVE ME DEATH!

92   REBEL WITHOUT A CLUTCH

## SIMPSONS #14

101   TO HEIR I$ HOMER

122   ITCHY & SCRATCHY
THIS BLOOD'S FOR YOU

124   NOSTALGIA AIN'T WHAT
IT USED TO BE

# A WARNING...

The contents of this book are under pressure. This is your first warning. Keep tightly closed in a cool, dry place. Do not point at face. Shake well before using. Batteries not included. Do not shake this book excessively. May cause drowsiness. All sales final. Intentional misuse of this book will render warranty void. Contents may have settled during shipping. Do not read this book by an open flame. This is your second warning. For external use only. Keep hands inside vehicle at all times. Harmful if swallowed. Watch for falling rocks. Rinse and repeat. Do not back up over this book—severe tire damage may result. Apply ointment sparingly. Do not remove this page under penalty of law. Report all suspicious activity to authorities immediately. Do not puncture or throw this book in fire. All shoplifters will be prosecuted. This is your final warning. Keep out of reach of impressionable adults. Complaints? Dial 1-555-EAT-MY-SHORTS. You have been warned.

MATT GROENING
Bongo Comics Group

# NED FLANDERS' TOP FORTY

## "THESE ARE A FEW OF MY FAVORITE THINGS"

1. Family togetherness nights.

2. My "better half"..."the ol' ball 'n' chain. (Hee hee, just kiddin', Maude!)

3. Yellow ribbons on oak trees.

4. My new Lawn Begone MX-7 GrassMaster tractor-mower.

5. **Bob Hope specials.**

6. Pants with just a skosh more room in the seat and thighs.

7. The impassioned rhetoric of Reverend Lovejoy.

8. Halogen lighting.

9. Stick-to-itiveness.

10. My new AudioCratic 48-disc CD player with fully uncontrollable no-access random play.

11. Yellow ribbons on flagpoles.

12. **Natural law.**

13. Waiters who introduce themselves.

14. The Ice Capades.

15. The heady mixture of politics and religion.

16. **Florence Henderson.**

17. Cordless power tools.

18. Traditional American Family Values.

19. Feelin' groovy.

20. Those new, super-tasty low-sodium snack foods.

21. Talking with "The Man Upstairs."

22. **My new 64-inch drive-in screen TV.**

23. Yellow ribbons on car antennas.

24. Theme restaurants.

25. The power of positive thinking.

26. **That cozy way my jogging suit feels when it's fresh out of the dryer.**

27. Quality time with Todd and Rod.

28. My new HeartAttacker-2000 deluxe Step-Meister exerciser.

29. Dinner theatre.

30. The simple satisfaction of a job well done.

31. The jazzy song stylings of La Streisand.

32. **Made-for-TV movies.**

33. Maude's meatloaf.

34. Good ol' American know-how.

35. War movies with dance music soundtracks.

36. *Reader's Digest*'s "Life in These United States."

37. **My new WeedBeater cordless Weasel-Wacker.**

38. Letting my inner-child out to play.

39. Yellow ribbons on high-voltage utility poles.

40. **Spunk.**

PLEASE, NED! SUCH *LANGUAGE*, IN FRONT OF *THE CHILDREN*! NOW WHAT DID I DO THAT WAS SO *TERRIBLE*?

OH, COME ON, MOTHER! YOU KNOW *DARNED* WELL THAT YOU CAN'T MAKE *S'MORES* WITHOUT DEEELICIOUS *CHOCOLATE*, AND *YOU* FORGOT TO *BRING* IT!

GRAMMIES

MARSH MELLOWS

WELL, JUST SANDWICH THE *MARSHMALLOWS* BETWEEN THE *GRAHAM CRACKERS* AND CALL IT SOMETHING *ELSE*!

BLASPHEMY!!

A FLANDERS CAMPEROONIE WITHOUT S'MORES IS LIKE...LIKE CHRISTMAS WITHOUT *FIGGY PUDDING*!

:SIGH: NED, WHERE ARE YOU GOING?!

I NEED TO BLOW OFF SOME STEAM. I'M GOING TO FIND MYSELF A NICE PIECE OF *KNOTTY PINE* AND DO SOME HARDCORE *WHITTLING*!!

AUGUST 31, 2:47 PM.

NOW NOW, MAUDE. THREE WEEKS ISN'T *THAT* LONG FOR NED TO BE MISSING. REMEMBER, THE LORD WORKS IN HIS OWN *TIME!*

HE'S RIGHT. AN EXPERIENCED JUNIOR CAMPER LEADER COULD LIVE FOR *WEEKS* IN THESE WOODS. THERE'S A WHOLE FOREST FULL OF NUTS AND BERRIES OUT THERE AND MOST OF THEM AREN'T ALL *THAT* POISONOUS!

⦂SOB! SNIFF⦂ I HAVEN'T GIVEN UP HOPE. IT'S JUST THAT WE HAD AN A-R-G-U-M-E-N-T THAT NIGHT AND I FEEL LIKE IT'S ALL *MY* FAULT!

DON'T BLAME *YOURSELF,* MA'AM. WE ALL HAVE OUR FAMILY SQUABBLES. AND NED DID THE RIGHT THING BY TAKING TIME OUT TO *COOL OFF.* THINGS COULD HAVE GOTTEN VERY UGLY.

HI, DADDY! CAN I GO FOR A SWIM WHILE THEY LOOK FOR THE *DEAD GUY?*

⦂GASP⦂

WHY YOU LITTLE...

HEH, HEH! DON'T BE ALARMED. JUST A BIT OF *FIRM* PARENTING. I SAW A FATHER DO THIS TO HIS SON ON T.V.

SIR, WE *FOUND* SOMETHING IN THE *HIGH GRASS!*

WHAT *IS* IT, RANGER?!

HEAVENS TO *BETSY*...

CLUNK!

IT'S A GIANT *COCKTAIL TOOTHPICK!*

IT'S A SIGN FROM *GOD!*

IT'S ONE OF NED'S *WHITTLE STICKS!*

ARTS AND CRAFTS MEANT *EVERYTHING* TO HIM. HE'D NEVER ABANDON HIS *STICK!*

OKEY DOKEY

WELL, THAT'S *THAT!* NOW GET ME OUTTA THIS GOD FORSAKEN *HELL HOLE*, BEFORE IT GETS DARK AND THE *SQUIRREL-RAVAGED CARCASS OF NED FLANDERS* RISES FROM THE DEAD AND COMES AFTER US SEEKING *REVENGE*...

FWAP!

UH, HEH, HEH! I MEAN, UH, WHO'S UP FOR A BITE TO EAT?

I BELIEVE A *CONCILIATORY PRAYER* IS IN ORDER. BUT FIRST, I MUST *ANNOINT* MYSELF WITH *OIL!*

EASY BAKE SPF-2

OH MIGHTY RA...ER, I MEAN, DEAR HEAVENLY FATHER--

*NED*, MY DARLING, WHERE *ARE* YOU?!

DON'T BE SO *SURE*, MOM! HE COULD BE A *FLESH-EATING ZOMBIE!*

D'OH! I *KNEW* IT WAS TOO GOOD TO BE *TRUE!*

DOES THIS MEAN I DON'T GET TO KEEP HIS *MOTOR HOME?*

HOMER, HIS *FAMILY* STILL OWNS *THAT!*

*WAP!*

*GEE WILLIKERS, MI FAMILIA!* IF I KNEW I'D GET *THIS* KIND OF WELCOME, I'D HAVE GOTTEN LOST IN THE WOODS *BEFORE!*

OH, *DADDY!* WE MISSED YOU *SO MUCH!*

GOLLY, LISTEN TO MY *RUMBLEDY-RUMBLER!* I'M SO HUNGRY I COULD EAT A *WHOLE* BOX OF COMMUNION WAFERS!

*RRRRRRRRRG!*

*JUUUST KIDDING!!!*

WHAT'S *WRONG,* SIS?

BART, DO YOU NOTICE ANYTHING *DIFFERENT* ABOUT *NED FLANDERS?*

YEAH! *P.U.!* THE GUY *STINKS!*

*EXACTLY!* REMEMBER WHEN THE CHURCH HAD THAT FUNDRAISER, *"GET GRITTY FOR GOD?"* HE WENT FOR *FORTY DAYS AND FORTY NIGHTS* WITHOUT TAKING A BATH, AND STILL SMELLED *DAISY FRESH!*

HMMMM, I WONDER...

DEAR DIARY, TODAY I WILL STRAY FROM TELLING YOU MY INNERMOST THOUGHTS AND FEELINGS BECAUSE I BELIEVE BART AND I HAVE UNCOVERED SOMETHING TRULY MYSTERIOUS, AND I JUST *HAVE* TO TELL YOU ABOUT IT.

EVER SINCE NED FLANDERS'S RETURN TO CIVILIZATION, WE'VE NOTICED A STRIKING *CHANGE* IN HIS PERSONALITY.

URRP!

MOST OF THE NEIGHBORS ARE BLAMING HIS BEHAVIOR ON *POST TRAUMATIC STRESS SYNDROME.* HOWEVER, BART AND I AREN'T CONVINCED.

I'M WITH STUPID

I SUPPOSE WANDERING AIMLESSLY THROUGH THE WOODS FOR WEEKS WITHOUT HUMAN CONTACT WOULD CAUSE EVEN THE MOST *DEVOUT* MAN TO GO A *LITTLE* INSANE...

GIVE ME THAT ICE CREAM CONE, LITTLE YOUNGSTER!

*WOOHOO!* WAY TO GO, FLANDERS!

HE'S TAKEN THE TIME-HONORED TRADITION OF STEALING CANDY FROM A BABY AND GIVEN IT A BRAND NEW TWIST!

YOINK!

WAPPETTA-WAPPETTA-WAPPETTA!

...BUT NED FLANDERS ALWAYS SEEMED *DIFFERENT!*

HIS FAITH ALWAYS SEEMED TO GIVE HIM THE POWER TO OVERCOME SUCH EMOTIONAL OBSTACLES.

HEY, KIDDLEY-DEES! ENJOY YOUR FREE TIME WHILE YOU *CAN!* DON'T LET THE FACT THAT *SCHOOL* STARTS *TOMORROW* RUIN YOUR LAST DAY OF *FREEDOM!*

IT WAS OBVIOUS THAT *SOMEONE* OR *SOMETHING* WAS AFFECTING HIM. SURE, IT MAY HAVE BEEN OVEREXPOSURE TO SOME ULTRA-CONSERVATIVE *RADIO PERSONALITY,* OR POSSIBLY LACK OF *FIBER* IN HIS *DIET.* BUT I'M WILLING TO BET IT WAS DUE TO SOME KIND OF *UNEXPLAINED PHENOMENON.*

FOR A GOOD TIME, CALL MAUDE

EVEN *I* WOULDN'T GO *THAT* FAR!

YET!

WHAT WILL FLANDERS DO *NEXT?*

SEPT. 14, 3:40 PM - *THE TOKYO NATIONAL BANK OF SPRINGFIELD.*

BRRIING!

STOP HIM! HELP! WE'VE BEEN ROBBED!

*OKILLY-DOKILLY,* EVERYBODY! THIS IS A *STICK-UP.* START SINGING LIL' RABBIT FOO FOO, AND NO ONE WILL GET *HURT!*

AND I WANT THE *LONG* VERSION!

TODAY'S BREAKFAST CONSISTS OF EGG WHITES, CARBO BOOST, WHEAT GRASS, SEAWEED, AND YOUR OWN *SECRET INGREDIENT*.

MMM...*HIGH FRUCTOSE CORN SYRUP!*

HERE ARE YOUR *MORNING PAPERS*, SIR. I BELIEVE YOU'LL FIND TODAY'S INSTALLMENT OF *DRABBLE* PARTICULARLY AMUSING.

GLOMP!

{SIGH} IT'S JUST *NOT* DA SAME SINCE DEY CANCELLED *FUNKY WINKAHBEAN!*

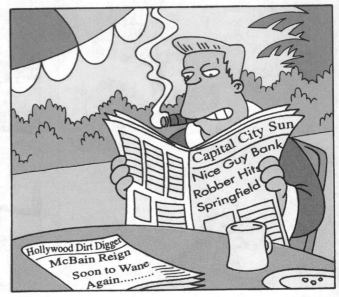

Capital City Sun

Nice Guy Bank Robber Hits Springfield

Hollywood Dirt Digget
McBain Reign Soon to Wane Again..........

WHAT DA...?!

GREEN GOOP

IS SOMETHING WRONG, SIR?

A FEW MONTHS AGO I HAD A *RUN-IN* WIT SOME *GREEN-BLOODED GUYS* LIKE DIS!* GAS UP DA HUMMER!

*SEE SIMPSONS #7 IF YOU DON'T BELIEVE HIM!

SEPT. 16, 11:20 AM.

BART, THERE ARE *"MCBAIN"* FLYERS ALL OVER TOWN WITH *OUR ADDRESS* ON THEM! WHAT ARE YOU *DOING*?!

WELCOME TO THE FIRST ANNUAL BART SIMPSON *MCBAIN-ATHON!* TWENTY-FOUR HOURS OF GUT-BURSTING, HEAD-CRUNCHING, BULLET-RIDDEN ACTION, VOID OF ANY STORYLINE AND *JAM-PACKED* WITH LAME-BUT-MEMORABLE ONE-LINERS. I FIGURED SINCE I RENTED SO MANY TAPES, I'D TRY TO RECOUP MY EXPENSES.

AND IF I DON'T PAY?!

KA-BASH!

OOPS!

RT WING

YOWZAH! DOES THAT ANSWER YOUR QUESTION?

SORRY ABOUT DAT. I HAVEN'T CHANGED THE BRAKES SINCE *DESERT STORM!*

MCBAIN, WHAT ARE YOU DOING IN *SPRINGFIELD!* AND MORE IMPORTANTLY, WHAT ARE YOU DOING IN THE MIDDLE OF OUR *LIVING ROOM?*

PLEASE, CALL ME *RAINIER!* I CAME TO INVESTIGATE DA WIMPY *BANK ROBBER* WIT DA *GREEN BLOOD!*

THEN I SAW DA MCBAIN SIGNS WIT DA ARROWS, AND FOLLOWED DEM *HERE!*

SEPT. 16, 12:05 PM - *KRUSTYBURGER STORE #37.*

≅SIGH≅... I CAN'T BELIEVE MY MODEL OF MALE MACHISMO IS EATING A *VEGETARIAN KRUSTY MIDWAY MEAL!*

IT'S DA ONLY WAY TO GET DA FREE TOY!

SO ANYWAY, THIS IS A *SAMPLE* OF THE *GREEN GOO* THAT TRICKLED OUT OF *NED FLANDERS'S BODY!*

MMM... LOOKS LIKE *GUACAMOLE!*

AFTER A THOROUGH MICROSCOPIC ANALYSIS, WE DETERMINED THAT THE FLUID IS COMPOSED OF CHEMICALS OF AN *UNEARTHLY NATURE!*

GOOD! I LIKE *NATURE!*

HUMOR HIM.

PSST! DON'T TURN AROUND! I'M HERE TO LIGHTEN YOUR LOAD!

≅GULP≅ ARE YOU FROM THE *IRS?* I SWEAR, DA SKI TRIP TO GSTAAD WAS *WORK-RELATED!*

GO WHERE FLANDERS *DISAPPEARED,* AND LOOK FOR SOMETHING *VERY WEIRD!*

AAH, *CRYPTIC MESSAGES!* BUT WE DON'T EVEN KNOW WHERE THE CAMPSITE *IS!*

I'LL ASK FOR *DIRECTIONS!*

RRRIIIP

IF MY CALCULATIONS ARE CORRECT, NED FLANDERS DISAPPEARED IN *THIS IMMEDIATE AREA.* OUR MYSTERY TIPSTER SAID TO LOOK FOR SOMETHING *WEIRD,* BUT *I* DON'T SEE ANYTHING *UNUSUAL!*

GOTTA...*REST!* CAN'T...GO...ANY ...*FURTHER!*

*WUMP!*

UH-OH, WHAT'S WRONG WIT THE LITTLE *PACK BOY?*

ASIDE FROM BEING *DEHYDRATED,* I BELIEVE MY BROTHER HAS DRAWN OUR ATTENTION TO AN *IMPORTANT CLUE!*

WE SEEM TO BE IN SOME KIND OF STRANGE *MATTED GRASSY AREA!*

BIG *DEAL!* I GOT A WHOLE *YAHD* LIKE DIS FROM MY *POOCH* DOING HIS *BUSINESS!*

I SAY WE SEND *MR. TOUGH GUY* UP A TREE FOR A *BETTER LOOK!* OR IS HE AFRAID HE MIGHT GET HIS *NAILS* DIRTY?!

HOW'D YOU LIKE A CLOSER LOOK AT MY NAILS WHEN I WRAP MY *FINGERS* AROUND YOUR PUNY LITTLE *THROAT?!*

¿GULP¡ I SUDDENLY HAVE A STRANGE *URGE* TO HUG SOME *BARK!*

SOON...

WELL BART, WHAT DO YOU *SEE*?!

RAINIER HAS A *BALD SPOT*!

I SHAVED IT FOR A ROLE THEY OFFERED *CONNERY*!

¦GASP¦ UH-OH! I *THINK* WE'RE IN TROUBLE!

WHAT *IS* IT, BART?!

DO YOU SEE *MARIA*?

SIDESHOW BOB!!

YOU WERE EXPECTING *E.T.?* GOOD OF YOU TO COME, BART. I AM SO LOOKING *FORWARD* TO DISINTEGRATING YOUR PUNY LITTLE BODY, *BONE* BY *BONE!*

WHO ARE YOUR *FRIENDS,* BOB?

OH, FORGIVE ME FOR BEING SO *RUDE.* MAY I INTRODUCE *KANG* AND *KODOS*-- TWO ALIENS WITH MORE FREQUENT FLYER MILES THAN ANYONE ON *RIGEL-4!*

HA! FLYER MILES! HA-HA!

KANG, IF ONLY ONE OF OUR *BRETHREN* HAD HAD THE JOCULAR ABILITY OF *BROTHER SIDESHOW,* WE'D BE LAUGHING FOR *ALL MILLENIUM!!*

YAH, HE'S A REGULAR *JERRY LEWIS!*

I THOUGHT YOU WERE IN *JAIL,* BOB.

I *WAS!* QUITE COMFORTABLE, TOO, UNTIL THAT BUFFOON *CANKER* HELPED ME ESCAPE.* FORTUNATELY, I WAS LUCKY ENOUGH TO BE *ABDUCTED* BY MY CHARMING ONE-EYED *HOSTS!*

CHECK OUT BARTMAN #4.

AT THE TIME, THEY WERE KIDNAPPING *HUMAN SPECIMENS* AND CREATING EVIL CLONE-LIKE *DUPLICATES* TO DEPOSIT BACK ON EARTH. THEY WANTED TO MAKE *ME* THEIR *NEXT* SUBJECT, HOWEVER, FINDING IT IMPOSSIBLE TO IMPROVE ON *PERFECTION,* I TOLD THEM...

♪ I'VE GOTTA BE *MEEE!!!* ♪

HOORAY! BRAVO!

ALL OF RIGEL-4 REVERE THE COCKNEY SONG STYLINGS OF *ANTHONY NEWLEY!*

AFTER I WOWED THEM WITH MY ONE-MAN PERFORMANCE OF *"STOP THE WORLD I WANT TO GET OFF"*, THEIR EVIL CLONE TECHNOLOGY WAS AT *MY* DISPOSAL!

LOCATING *NED FLANDERS*, I IMMEDIATELY ABDUCTED HIM FROM HIS CAMPSITE, IN HOPES THAT AN *EVIL FLANDERS CLONE* COULD BE PROGRAMMED TO MURDER A CERTAIN *ANNOYING LITTLE NEIGHBOR*. I WOULD HAVE MY REVENGE ON YOU, BART, AND, OF COURSE, NONE OF THIS COULD BE TRACED BACK TO *MOI!*

A PITY, THE CLONE *DISAPPEARED* BEFORE BRINGING MY PLAN TO *FRUITION!*

A MEANINGLESS GAME WE PLAY WHEN WE'RE BORED. SORT OF A RIGELLIAN VERSION OF *TIC-TAC-TOE!*

AND WHAT ABOUT THE *CROP CIRCLES?*

THE *RED BUTTON* ON THE CONSOLE CONTROLS *EVERYTHING!* WHEN WE DISCOVERED YOUR LITTLE SEARCH PARTY, I CREATED THE *"NO BART"* GRAPHIQUE IN AN EFFORT TO DRAW YOU INTO AN ABDUCTABLE LOCATION.

NOW IT APPEARS I'M GOING TO HAVE TO ELIMINATE YOU *MYSELF!* HOW DO YOU FEEL ABOUT *PRE-DEATH EMBALMING,* BART?!

EEEP!

DON'T *WORRY,* BART. I'VE GOT AN *IDEA!*

WRROOOOOO

ACH! WHAT IN TH' NAME O' *NESSIE...?* SOUNDS LIKE THE *WAILIN'* OF A *BANSHEE!*

SCOTSMEN FIGHT LIKE WEE LASSIES

DAG BLAST YE NO GOOD *SPACE BLAGGARDS!* I'LL TEACH YE WHAT A *SCOTSMAN* KIN *DYOOO!!*

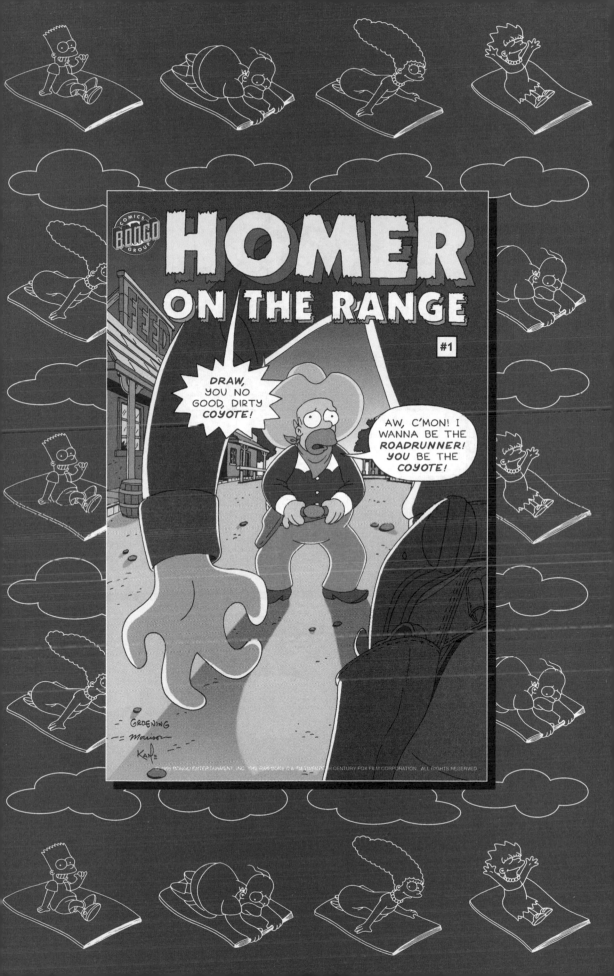

KIDS TODAY GET TOO MUCH VIOLENCE FROM TV AND MOVIES. BACK IN MY DAY IT WAS *RIGHT OUTSIDE* YOUR *WINDOW*, AND YOU COULD EXPERIENCE IT ON A NICE SUMMER DAY. BUT THAT WAS A TIME WHEN JUSTICE RODE A HORSE NAMED *VIOLENCE*. NO, I DON'T THINK JUSTICE HAD A HORSE BACK THEN, HE COULDN'T *AFFORD* IT. EVEN THOUGH LIFE WAS CHEAPER; YOU COULD GET A SARSAPARILLA FOR *A PENNY* AT THE OLD DRY GOODS STORE. IT REMINDS ME OF A STORY...

# THE KWIK-E AND THE DEAD!

IN 1897, *TROUBLE* CAME TO SPRINGFIELD. *JEBEDIAH* COULDN'T HAVE KNOWN THAT THE TOWN HE FOUNDED RESTED ON A *GIANT OIL FIELD*. WILDCAT INDUSTRIALIST, *MONTGOMERY BURNS,* STAKED A CLAIM TO THE OIL DEPOSIT, AND THE IRON HORSE, GUNFIGHTERS, AND SOME FELLA SELLING FISH 'N' CHIPS FOLLOWED HIM INTO TOWN...

MOE'S SALOON

HORSE SPURS-N-SUCH 'R' US

WESTERN STUFF BANK

I TELL YA', THERE'S SOMETHIN' *ODD* 'BOUT THAT INDIAN.

WELL, AT LEAST HE AIN'T *TROUBLE* LIKE BURNS AND HIS RUFFIANS.

OUTSIDE THE SALOON...

WHINNIE

CLOP! CLOP! CLOP!

MY FRIEND *NEW SHERIFF*, I WILL BE GIVING YOU THIS *GUN* TO PROTECT FIRST *MY STORE* AND THEN THE TOWN.

WHY, THANK YOU, CHIEF, ER -- I MEAN, THANK YOU, MY *NATIVE-AMERICAN FRIEND*.

WHY DOES NO ONE *LISTEN?*... I AM NOT *THAT* KIND OF INDIAN.

WELL, WHERE IS THAT STAR-CLAD, WHIMPERING WEASEL? *SMITTY!* HELP ME WITH MY SIX-SHOOTER.

*RIGHT AWAY*, SIR.

SHERIFF, TO SHOW OUR APPRECIATION FOR YOUR *BRAVERY*, I MADE YOU THIS *PIE*.

MMM, *PIE!*

I'LL JUST PUT IT HERE FOR LATER.

33

NO ONE IS REALLY SURE WHAT HAPPENED NEXT, AND I DON'T EVEN REMEMBER IF I WAS *ACTUALLY THERE*. IN FACT, I MAY NOT HAVE EVEN BEEN *ALIVE* YET. BUT, THE CITIZENS OF SPRINGFIELD FOUND COURAGE FROM THE SACRIFICE OF THE NEW SHERIFF, EVEN THOUGH HE WAS *DEAD*. I THINIK THEY WERE OFF THEIR NUTS. THEY SHOULD HAVE LET BURNS TAKE OVER THE TOWN. I BET THERE WOULDN'T BE SO MANY STRIP MALLS NOW IF EVERYONE HAD CAVED INTO BURNS BACK THEN. BUT *NOOO*, THEY HAD TO REBEL...

YOU SHOT THE SHERIFF, BUT YOU DIDN'T SHOOT HIS NEW *DEPUTY*!

OR ME!

OR *ME*!

OR *ME*!

LET'S *GET* 'EM!

RUN, SMITTY, IT'S A PROLETARIAT UPRISING!

HEAR ME, *SPRINGFIELD*, YOU HAVE NOT HEARD THE *LAST* OF MONTGOMERY BURNS!...

MMM, CHERRY.

...I'LL *OWN* THIS TOWN! MAYBE NOT TODAY, BUT SOMEDAY YOU'LL ALL BE WORKING FOR *MEEEE*!

THE BULLET HIT THE *PIE TIN*!

GOOD FRIEND NEW SHERIFF, YOU ARE *ALIVE*.

OH, I DON'T KNOW WHAT I'M TALKING ABOUT ANYMORE. STUPID TV FILLS YOUR MIND WITH *MARBLES*. THAT REMINDS ME OF WHEN THEY BROUGHT THE *OLYMPICS* TO SPRINGFIELD BACK IN '23, OR WAS THAT '32?... HMMM, COULD'VE BEEN TIDDLY-WINKS ...I GUESS.

THE END

STORY W.E. HOLLIDAY   PENCILS LUIS ESCOBAR   INKS TIM HARKINS & TIM BAVINGTON   LETTERING MIKE SAKAMOTO   COLOR NATHAN KANE   MAN WITH NO NAME MATT GROENING

### PING PONG SET

Comes complete with one paddle, one ball, and official rule book. All you need is another paddle, net, and table for hours of ping pong fun.

### "SWISHER JET"
**Ready-to-fly jet aeroplane!**

Nothing to build. Just attach wings, light fuse, and away it goes. Flies at least 9 ft. Works only once!

### INCREDIBLE PROFESSIONAL GUITAR

Miniature. Shiny. Beautiful tone. Not a ukulele. Plays "Turkey in the Straw." All you do is turn the little crank.

### SCIENTIFIC CHEMISTRY SET

Complete with several chemicals, including salt, sugar and $H_2O$. Comes with science napkin, science spoon, and science cup.

### REALISTIC WRIST WATCH

For boys and girls. Needs no winding. Handsome. Just like grown-ups wear. Pretend to tell time. Hands seem to move if you jiggle watch really hard.

### Official Size  Official Weight
### PROFESSIONAL BASKETBALL

Well, not really. Actually, an orange-colored gumball, approx. 1/4 in. in diameter. Tasty.

### BIG CATCH FISHING OUTFIT

This great outfit includes 3-1/2 ft. hickory stick, string, paper-clip-style hook. Plus bonus dried worm.

### DINK-E-CRAFT MICROSCOPE OUTFIT

Precision-built. Complete with lens. See crumbs, dots, and specks. Don't miss. Make discoveries.

### RADIO KIT

A genuine radio. Build it. Listen to it. Hear that crackle? That's called static!

### JR. BEAVER AXE KIT

All-purpose kit. Looks like plain old hammer in disguise. Just sharpen it till the hammer head wears down to "axe-like" look.

## I'M "UNCLE" KRUSTY

# I WILL SEND YOU PRIZES LIKE THESE*

*Not these prizes, exactly, but prizes somewhat like these*

Hiya, kids! I have been helping boys and girls just like you get prizes for 17 years, except for that brief time I spent in jail when I got framed by Sideshow Bob, and those two other times when I got nabbed for tax evasion. Anyway, where was I? Oh yeah—shown here are just a few of the wonderful prizes you might get for selling my famous Krusty Brand exotic Flower Seed Packs. Just between you and me, these so-called exotic flower seeds are really just annoying milkweed seeds—heh heh—but don't tell the customers that! Believe me, the truth just ain't good for business! So here's where you come in. Any of the prizes on this page can be yours if you just sell 3 cases of 87 boxes of 40 packs of seeds at the low, low price of $1.89 a pack. Many youngsters sell their packs in 1 day and get their prizes before they know it, and that's a "Krusty Promise."*
*Not a real promise.

### HURRY! BE THE 1ST IN YOUR NEIGHBORHOOD

Get in early before the grown-ups find out these so-called flower seeds are nothing but nuisance weeds! Do whatever you gotta do to sell these seed packs! Turn on the charm, threaten, cajole, even throw tantrums. Grandparents are expecially gullible to whining and guilt trips! You'll sell your seed packs quickly to your family, friends, and neighbors! Just send me the cash! Don't forget the cash! Remember: Send me that cash!

### SEND VERY LITTLE MONEY—I TRUST YOU—AND YOU TRUST ME. RIGHT?

Prize Winner Milhouse Van Houton says: "I sold 3,584 packs of seeds and got a little rubber doggie. It's not the prize I wanted, but Krusty says if I sell a lot more seeds, maybe I'll get something better."

### BOW AND ARROW ARCHERY SET

Includes little bow, really little arrow, and really really little target. Just like the elves use.

### FLASH CAMERA

This spiffy outfit takes blurry, out-of-focus "artistic" shots. Wow!! Be the next famous big-time photographer like whatsisname.

### HERE IT IS—THE GOLDEN "TRUMPET"

Over 5 inches long. Play bugle calls, hot bebop, Top 40 hits. Works on unique "kazoo" principle. Fool your friends, self.

### EVER-SO-PRETTY TRAVEL CASE

Overnight case with removable tray. Comes with mirror shard, key. No lock. Stores one pack of gum or two little pink erasers.

### ROMANTIC LOCKET SET

Gorgeous necklace with locket that opens if you pry hard enough. Elegant and swell.

## EXTRA! $50
### IN GRAND PRIZES

**1st PRIZE** Mystery Box
**2nd PRIZE** Surprise Package
**3rd PRIZE** Leaky Grab Bag

You are eligible to win if you sell at least 1,000 seed packs.

**PLUS 20 Official SIDESHOW MEL USED UNICYCLES!**

## MAIL THIS NOW—*AND I MEAN NOW!*

"Uncle" Krusty the Clown, KRUSTY SEED CO., Box B, Dept. RM, SPRINGFIELD USA

Please send me 3 cases of 87 boxes of 40-pack seeds. I will re-sell them and send you all the money and choose my prize. Enclosed is $5 initiation fee, $10 processing fee, $35 deposit, and $7.50 for postage and handling. All seeds delivered C.O.D.

Name_____

Address_____

Town_____Zone_____State_____

Offer void after Sept. 15, 1968.

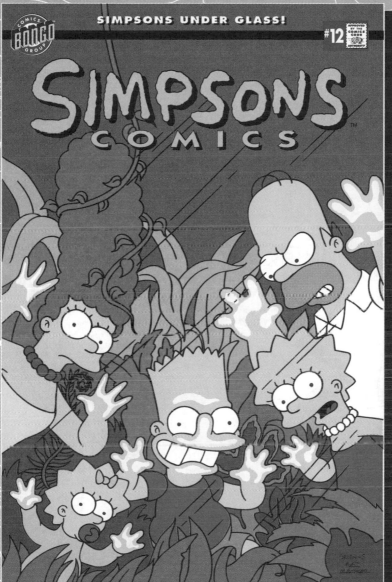

# SURVIVAL of the FATTEST!

DESTRUCTION! BLOOD! WAR! TERROR HAS STRUCK *EVERYWHERE*!!

BAM!

| SCRIPT ROB HAMMERSLEY & TODD J. GREENWALD | PENCILS ERIC MOXCEY | INKS TIM BAVINGTON | LETTERING MIKE SAKAMOTO | COLOR ELECTRIC CRAYON | CLIMATE CONTROLLER MATT GROENING |

...ENOUGH ABOUT MY BITTER DIVORCE. NOW THE NEWS... AFTER A LONG AND EXHAUSTIVE SELECTION PROCESS, SPRINGFIELD HAS BEEN CHOSEN AS THE SITE OF THE NEXT ENVIRONMENTAL RESEARCH BIOSPHERE. WE GO TO THE SCENE JUST MINUTES AGO.

...SPRINGFIELD.

WHAT ARE YOUR THOUGHTS ON THE BIOSPHERE COMING TO SPRINGFIELD?

HI, MOM! I'M ON TV! UURRP!

A BIMBO-SPHERE! WOO-HOO! IT'S ABOUT TIME THIS TOWN GOT ANOTHER STRIP JOINT!

NO, DAD, IT'S A BIOSHPERE -- A SCIENCE EXPERIMENT.

HUH?

A SELF-CONTAINED ANIMATED ENVIRONMENT.

HUH?

IT'S SORT OF LIKE A HUMAN HABITRAIL.

OH, I GET IT.

HI, I'M TROY MCCLURE! YOU MAY REMEMBER ME FROM SUCH SCIENCE PROJECTS AS *OPERATION LICE* AND *CONDOS ON MARS!* BUT TODAY I'M HERE TO WELCOME THE BIOSPHERE TO SPRINGFIELD! ONE LUCKY FAMILY WILL BE CHOSEN TO SPEND A GLORIOUS YEAR IN OUR LUXURIOUS, STATE OF THE ART BIOSPHERE.

ONCE INSIDE, YOU GET TO EXPERIENCE ALL OF OUR EXOTIC CLIMATES, INCLUDING THE *DESERT REGION*...

THE *TROPICAL RAIN FOREST*...

...AND MANY MORE! YOU'LL LIVE OFF THE LAND AND ENJOY ALL THAT NATURE HAS TO OFFER.

WACK!

FLUMPH!

PLUS, YOU WON'T HAVE TO WORRY ABOUT THE DAY-TO-DAY HASSLES OF THE OUTSIDE WORLD.

SOUND ENTICING? I THOUGHT SO. BUT THAT'S NOT ALL! IF YOUR FAMILY IS CHOSEN, WE'LL PAY YOU *FIFTY THOUSAND PESOS!*

FIFTY THOUSAND PESOS! WOOHOO!!

THAT IS ALL WE'LL BE NEEDING FROM YOU TODAY. TAKE YOUR SCORECARD TO THE REGISTRATION DESK.

BUT WHAT ABOUT THE OTHER TESTS?

I'VE SEEN JUST ABOUT **ALL** I NEEDED TO SEE.

THE RESULTS WILL BE ANNOUNCED ON TV *TONIGHT*.

Chances of Survival 0%

HOW'D WE DO, DAD?

Chances of Survival 100%

WE DID *GREAT!* YOU SHOULD BE *PROUD* TO BE A SIMPSON.

THAT NIGHT...

VE ARE PROUD TO ANNOUNCE DAT THERE VERE *TWO* FAMILIES DAT SCORED PERFECTLY ON OUR EXAMS. SO, VE SELECTED ZEM *BOTH*. FIRST, ZE *HOMER SIMPSON* FAMILY.

BIOSPHERE

PRESS CONFERENCE

YES! WE'RE *NUMBER ONE!*

UND ZE *NED FLANDERS* FAMILY.

AAAAAAAAAAHHHHHH!!!

SEVERAL DAYS LATER...

I HEREBY ANNOUNCE THE OFFICIAL *OPENING* AND, ER, *CLOSING* OF THE SPRINGFIELD BIOSPHERE!

POP!

PSSSSSSST!

AFTER A SPEEDY RECONSTRUCTION...

ENOUGH WITH THE CEREMONIAL MUMBO-JUMBO. GET YOUR *GUINEA PIG BUTTS* IN THERE.

KLUNK

LAST ONE TO BUILD THEIR HUT IS A ROTTEN *OINKELY-DOINKELY.*

*BUILD?* I THOUGHT THEY SAID ALL WE HAD TO DO IS PICK THE HUT WE WANTED.

YES-ER-OONY. YOU PICK THE HUT YOU WANT TO BUILD. IT'S ALL IN THIS HANDY-DANDY *SURVIVAL GUIDE* THEY GAVE US. WHERE'S YOURS?

BIO-GUIDE
THE DIFFERENCE BETWEEN LIFE AND DEATH

UH, I DIDN'T GET ONE.

WELL, IF YOU NEED ANY HELP MY USUAL NEIGHBORLY *HELPING HAND* IS GOOD RIGHT HERE IN THE BIOSPHERE.

LET'S GET ONE THING STRAIGHT HERE, FLANDERS. I CAN TAKE CARE OF *MY FAMILY* JUST FINE. THE LAST THING I NEED IS HELP FROM *YOU!*

YOUR BARN DOOR'S OPEN.

THANKS.

ZZIP!

LATER...

FINISHED! WELL, WHAT DO YOU KNOW, I'M *DONE* AND MR. HELPING HAND HASN'T EVEN *STARTED*.

SLICE!

SPA-DOING!

WOW, *SWEET PAD!*

BEGINNER'S LUCK.

EVEN LATER...

SINCE I SAW CHAKA DO IT ON "LAND OF THE LOST." NOW, I'LL GET SOME *BAMBOO CHUTES* AND YOU GET SOME *NEEDLES*.

BEHOLD – THE *MIGHTY LAMB*. SOON TO BE OUR BOUNTIFUL FEAST. ALL WE NEED TO DO IS MAKE A BLOWGUN.

SINCE WHEN DO *YOU* KNOW SO MUCH ABOUT HUNTING?

FIND A PORCUPINE, TICKLE ITS BELLY AND WHEN IT LAUGHS, TAKE SOME NEEDLES.

FIND, TICKLE, TAKE – CHECK.

AAAAAAAAAAAHHHHH!!!

HE DIDN'T THINK IT WAS FUNNY.

*GOOD JOB, BOY!* NOW WATCH AND LEARN. THE TRICK IS TO TAKE A DEEP BREATH.

PLUCK!

SHOONK!

AFTER ANOTHER UNSUCCESSFUL DAY...

OH, BOY. BANANA...*AGAIN*. WHAT ARE WE GOING TO DO TONIGHT, *KABOB* IT?

WHATEVER YOU DO, I'VE GOT DIBS ON THE PEEL.

HOMER, I HATE TO BE THE NEGATIVE ONE, BUT IT'S BEEN A *WEEK* NOW AND ALL WE'VE HAD TO EAT IS FIVE BANANAS AND A BUNCH OF STICKS.

HOW LONG CAN WE *SURVIVE* LIKE THIS?

SO WE'RE OFF TO A SLOW START. THESE BIOSPHERES TAKE A WHILE TO GET USED TO. YOU CAN'T EXPECT US TO LIVE HIGH OFF THE HOG IN THE *FIRST WEEK*.

QUE PASA, MI NEIGHBURRITOS! WE DECIDED TO GO MEXICAN TONIGHT. COME OVER AND GIVE THE OLD *PINATA* A WHACK.

TING LINGA-LING!

NO... AND THAT'S MEXICAN FOR *NO!*

HOMER, I THINK IT'S ABOUT TIME YOU LET NED *HELP* US. WE COULD WORK TOGETHER, SO WE CAN *ALL* ENJOY THIS EXPERIENCE.

YEAH, BECAUSE THIS SUCKS.

FLANDERS, I'M THE *KING* OF THIS FAMILY, AND IF THEY'RE GOING TO RELY ON ANYONE, IT'S GOING TO BE *ME!*

IF YOU CHANGE YOUR MIND, MI CASA ES *SU* CASA.

TOSS!

ZIP!

DON'T WORRY, WE'RE JUST *FINE*. WE'VE SURVIVED ONE WEEK; FIFTY-ONE MORE WON'T *KILL* US.

THAT NIGHT...

I'VE ALMOST GOT IT. I THINK I SEE SMOKE.

POP!

I *DID* IT! I SAID LET THERE BE FIRE, AND THERE WAS FIRE, AND IT WAS GOOD!

GEE, HOMEY, MAYBE I WAS A LITTLE TOO PREMATURE IN *DOUBTING* YOU.

POP!

SNAPPLE!

CROK!

WAY TO GO, DAD. THIS COULD BE A WHOLE NEW START FOR US.

ALL YOU *NAYSAYERS* DIDN'T BELIEVE IN ME. WELL, *THIS* WILL SHOW YOU...

WHOOOSH!

POP!

POP!

CRACK!

SIZZLE!

SIZZLE!

LET'S JUST GO TO SLEEP.

THE NEXT MORNING...

ACTIVITY UPDATE!

PLOOP!

SNOW ANGEL MAKING ON OUR FRONT YARD IN TEN TICKLY TICKS OF THE CLOCK!

KRAK!

DAD, WHEN WE'RE DONE, CAN I SHOVEL THE YARD?

NO FAIR, LAST NIGHT HE GOT TO CLEAN THE DISHES.

STOP QUARRELING, CHILDREN. THERE ARE ENOUGH CHORES TO GO AROUND FOR EVERYONE!

MOM, I CAN'T SEE. MY EYELIDS ARE FROZEN SHUT.

SO ARE MY NOSTRILS! IF I SNEEZE MY HEAD WILL EXPLODE!

HOMER, THE KIDS ARE MISERABLE AND I'M MISERABLE. I THINK WE SHOULD GO TO THE FLANDERS'S AND LET THEM HELP US.

COME ON, MARGE, DON'T LET A LITTLE FROSTBITE AND STARVATION GET YOU DOWN. IF YOU LEAVE, YOU'LL JUST BE TELLING ME THAT I'M NO GOOD.

LATER, HOMER.

SORRY, DAD.

WHEN YOU SWALLOW YOUR PRIDE, YOU KNOW WHERE WE'LL BE.

AFTER HOURS OF AIMLESS ROAMING...

WHY DID I EVER DO THIS *STUPID* BIOSPHERE THING? MY FAMILY HATES ME... I'M TOTALLY WORTHLESS... AND TO TOP IT ALL OFF, I HAVEN'T HAD A *BEER* IN TWO WEEKS. *TWO WEEKS!*

HOLY MOLY! IT'S TV'S TROY MCCLURE, STAR OF THE HIT FAMILY SERIES "TEN IS TOO MANY!" WHAT ARE *YOU* DOING HERE?

HOMER, I'M YOUR FANTASY.

THEN WHO'S THE *LOOKER?*

OH, SHE'S *MY* FANTASY.

I'LL CATCH UP WITH YOU LATER, TOOTS.

HOMER, I'VE HAD A LOT OF EXPERIENCE BEING A FATHER -- *ON TELEVISION*, OF COURSE. IN REAL LIFE I'M SURE I'VE FATHERED *DOZENS* OF THOSE LITTLE BAMBINOS.

BUT HECK, WHAT YOU DON'T KNOW CAN'T HURT YOU! I'M HERE TO HELP SO ASK ME *ANYTHING* YOU WANT.

OKAY.

*POOF!*

IS THAT KID WHO PLAYED YOUR SON STILL IN *JAIL?*

MAYBE YOU DON'T UNDERSTAND...

IF YOU HAD ANOTHER KID, WOULD THE SHOW BE CALLED "ELEVEN IS *WAY* TOO MANY?"

*HOMER!* QUESTIONS ABOUT *YOUR* FAMILY! YOU REMEMBER, THE ONES WHO *LEFT* YOU.

OH, RIGHT.

I WANT YOU TO SEE SOMETHING. COME HERE AND LOOK INTO MY *BLUE HA-WAIIAN.*

OOOH!

LAZARUS RISING FROM THE GRAVE?

JESUS HEALING THE BLIND?

SOME GEEK WEARING A SHEET CARRYING TWO BOOKS?

YOU'RE ALL WRONG. IT'S *MOSES* BRINGING DOWN THE TABLETS FROM ON HIGH.

AWWWW...

DON'T FRET A SWEAT. WE STILL HAVEN'T HIT THE *NEW* TESTAMENT YET.

NEW TESTAMENT

AWWWW...

OH, *NO*! HE'S *BRAINWASHING* THEM! MAKE IT STOP!

I CAN'T. BUT YOU CAN. YOU HAVE TO SHOW YOUR FAMILY YOU'RE *RESPONSIBLE* AND YOU CAN TAKE CARE OF THEM.

BUT I'M A *LOUSY* DAD. EVERYTHING I DO JUST BLOWS UP IN MY FACE.

HOMER, FOLLOW ME. I'M GOING TO HELP YOU.

MAINTENANCE

I'M GIVING YOU *TWO* OPTIONS. BEHIND THAT WATERFALL IS A WAY OUT OF THE BIOSPHERE. YOU CAN LEAVE, GIVE UP ON YOUR FAMILY AND LIVE YOUR LIFE *RIDDEN WITH GUILT.* OR YOU CAN STAY HERE, GO BACK TO YOUR FAMILY AND SHOW THEM THAT YOU'RE THE *BEST* FATHER YOU CAN BE.

HOMER, YOU'RE ON YOUR OWN NOW. IF YOU NEED ANY MORE HELP, JUST LISTEN TO YOUR *HEART.*

POP

WELL, HEART, I'M GOING BACK TO SPRINGFIELD. MY FAMILY WILL BE BETTER OFF *WITHOUT* ME.

STUPID BIOSPHERE! THIS THING WAS SUPPOSED TO BE *EASY!* I'M JUST A LOSER...WITH A CAPITAL *LOO!*

MEANWHILE...

YOU KNOW, I'M REALLY STARTING TO *WORRY* ABOUT YOUR FATHER.

ARTS AND CRAFTS IN TEN MINUTES!

YEAH, AND THIS HAPPY ROUTINE IS GETTING OLD FAST.

IF I HEAR ONE MORE VERSE OF KUM-BA-YAH, I'M GOING TO BEAT SOMEONE WITH A *HYMNAL.*

THE FLANDERS HAVE BEEN NICE ENOUGH TO LET US INTO THEIR HOME. I THINK THE *LEAST* WE CAN DO IS PRETEND TO ENJOY OURSELVES.

BUT WHAT ABOUT *DAD?*

I DON'T KNOW, LISA. MAYBE YOUR FATHER JUST NEEDS SOME TIME *ALONE.* BUT FOR NOW, YOU KIDS PUT ON HAPPY FACES AND GRAB YOUR SMOCKS.

THIS *BITES!*

SPAK!

HEADS I WALK -- TAILS I STAY.

FLIP!

MEANWHILE, BACK AT THE CASA DE FLANDERS...

PUFF.

PUFF.

SIZZLE! SIZZLE!

CRACKLE-CRACK!

THIS IS *IT!* THE BIGGEST DECISION OF MY *LIFE.* IF I LEAVE, I CAN GO HOME AND WATCH "SHE'S THE SHERIFF" RERUNS TILL MY EYES FALL OUT. OR IF I STAY, I CAN SUCK UP TO FLANDERS LIKE THE PATHETIC *BOOB* THAT I AM.

OKAY, TWO OUT OF THREE.

HEY, WHAT'S THAT *SMELL?*

JIMINY CHRISTMAS! THE HOUSE IS ABLAZE AND THE STAIRS ARE GONE! WE'RE *TRAPPED!*

*NED,* WHAT ARE WE GOING TO *DO?*

DIE!!!

OH, HOMER, I WAS SO *WORRIED* ABOUT YOU. I DIDN'T THINK YOU WERE GOING TO COME BACK.

I DIDN'T THINK SO EITHER, BUT I HAD A HEART TO HEART WITH MY HEART AND DECIDED THAT I'M NO LONGER GOING TO BE A FAT, LAZY, IRRESPONSIBLE FATHER. FROM NOW ON I'M GOING TO BE A FAT, LAZY, *RESPONSIBLE* FATHER!

WAY TO GO, HOMER!

DAD, YOU'RE THE BEST FATHER A KID COULD HAVE!

AND THE BEST HUBBY TOO!

WE'RE OUT! WE'RE SAVED! HOMER, YOU MUST BE *BLESSED.*

NAH, I JUST MADE A WISH UPON A *STAR.*

BIOSPHERE CANNED!
McCLURE SCANDAL
TEN WASN'T TOO MANY CLAIM 30 UNWED MOTHERS

THE END

...THEY WERE *HOOLIGANS* THAT NEEDED TO TAKE A TURN FROM *OBLIVION* ONTO THE FREEWAY OF THE *STRAIGHT AND NARROW!*

NOW RINSE AND REPEAT, PRIVATE!

BY THEN I KNEW THAT WAR *STINKS*, BUT I MADE SURE THAT THE PRIVATES IN MY COMPANY *DIDN'T!* MY BOYS BATHED TWICE A DAY!

I TAUGHT MY BOYS TO *FIGHT!*

WE CONDUCTED *GROOMING DRILLS!*

I WILL NOT TOLERATE *BEGRIMED NAILS* IN THIS MAN'S ARMY!

TO KEEP THEIR MINDS SHARP, I ADMINISTERED THE OCCASIONAL *VOCABULARY TEST.*

NOW, WHO AMONGST YOU LUNKS CAN PROPERLY USE THE TERM *GENRE?*

UH, IT'S A DISTINCTIVE TYPE OR CATEGORY, ESPECIALLY OF LITERARY COMPOSITION.

IN THE END, PUNISHMENT WAS DISHED OUT AS REGULARLY AS RATIONS...

PLOP!

...MY CREDO WAS *SPARE THE ROD, SPOIL THE GRUNT!*

IT MADE THEM INTO *SOLDIERS!* ALAS, MY BOYS DIDN'T SEE IT THAT WAY...

I'M SICK OF SHINING GRENADES.

*GRENADE DUTY?* I HAVE TO SANITIZE THE LAND MINES TONIGHT!

OF ALL THE OUTFITS IN THIS ARMY, I HAD TO LAND IN SERGEANT SEYMOUR SPIC'N'SPAN SKINNER'S.

I WAS MAILING A LETTER TO MOTHER WHEN I OVERHEARD THE BOYS TALKING.

HEE HEE! SNICKER! HAW HAW!

I TELL YA, FELLAS, THAT SKINNER IS A GRADE-A *EIGHTBALL*. THERE'S A *WAR* GOING ON AND HE'S BUSY MAKING US WAX OUR *KNEECAPS*!

THE ENEMY BETTER WATCH OUT! IF SKINNER CATCHES 'EM, HE MIGHT CUT THEIR HAIR!

HA HA HAW! HA HA HA!

CRUSHED, I RETURNED TO MY QUARTERS AND STEAM-CLEANED MY BOOTS. THE BOYS CONTINUED THEIR CHARCOALED REVELRY, WHEN ONE OF THE PRIVATES NOTICED SOMETHING IN THE NEARBY SHRUBBERY.

HEY, FELLAS, *LOOK*!

KRUSTY'S FAMOUSE SAUCE

YUM! IT'S BLUE!

CONDIMENTS FROM BACK HOME! *HOW*?!

I HAVEN'T SEEN A BOTTLE OF *KRUSTY'S FAMOUS* FOR *MONTHS*!

THERE'S MORE?

THERE'S MORE!

THE BOYS SCRAMBLED INTO THE JUNGLE FOR THE SAVORY SANDWICH DRESSINGS AND KETCHUPS, ROAMING FAR FROM CAMP IN THEIR MAD RUSH!

WHILE I MARTINIZED MY SOCKS, I HAD AN *EPIPHANY!* I DECIDED THAT I MUST TELL MY BOYS WHY *CLEANLINESS* WAS NEXT TO *GODLINESS!* WHY, A SOLDIER MUST BE BOTH A CRACK SHOT *AND* BANG-UP LATRINE DIGGER! BUT WHEN I RETURNED TO THE BARBECUE, I FOUND THEM...

GONE!

IT DIDN'T TAKE ME LONG TO FIGURE OUT WHAT HAD HAPPENED...

I HAD RECEIVED A MIMEOGRAPHED INTELLIGENCE REPORT ABOUT THE *CEYE-YUNG PRISONER CAMP* FORTY-FIVE CLICKS FROM THE BASE. I KNEW THAT IF THE BOYS HAD BEEN CAPTURED, THEY'D BE *THERE*.

I WAS RIGHT!

I SILENTLY CREPT INTO THE JUNGLE, USING MY COMB TO ERASE MY TRACKS, READY TO SPRING MY PLAN...

HEY, DO YOU SMELL SOMETHING?

I THINK IT'S...*OLD SPICE!*

YEAH... WHAT IS THAT?

LOOK!

RUSTLE!

RUSTLE!

SHIFT!

63

USING ITEMS FROM MY EXTENSIVE TOILETRY KIT, I CREATED A *WHOLE PLATOON!* THE NON-STAINING ANTIPERSPIRANT STICKS I SURROUNDED THE CAMP WITH GAVE THE ENEMY THE ODOR OF AN APPROACHING, OVERWHELMING FORCE!

THE TREES AND BUSHES I JERRY-RIGGED WITH MY NAIL CLIPPER, TOOTHBRUSH, DENTAL FLOSS, AND EAR WAX REMOVAL SYSTEM CREATED MY FAUX-PLATOON'S MARCH!

THOSE WHO TRIED TO RUN FELL INTO *LATRINE TRENCHES* I DUG AROUND THE CAMP!

SNIPERS LOOKING THROUGH THEIR SCOPES WERE BLINDED BY MY *ULTRA-SHINED HELMET!* I HAD TAKEN THE CAMP -- ON MY OWN -- USING THE SAME SKILLS I TRIED SO HARD TO IMBUE IN MY BOYS.

SOON, MY BOYS AND I TRANSFORMED THE P.O.W. COMPOUND INTO A *TRUE* DETENTION CAMP.

I will not practice Communist ideology
I will not practice Communist ideology
I will not practice Communist ideology
I will not p

UH, SIR?

YES?

SIR, ON BEHALF OF THE BOYS, I'D LIKE TO THANK YOU FOR WHAT YOU DID. YOUR SPIC'N'SPAN SOLDIERING SAVED OUR SORRY BUTTS.

UH SIR, COULD I BORROW YOUR *COMB?* I WOULDN'T WANT TO APPEAR *SLOVENLY.*

GO AHEAD, SOLDIER, BORROW MY COMB. BE SURE TO USE THE *FIELD BARBICIDE* I BROUGHT IN MY PACK.

# AS SEEN ON "SMARTLINE"

## WHAT ARE YOU, NUTS OR SOMETHING?

Unwind your mind and leave your troubles behind at

# Dr. Marvin Monroe's
# E-Z ANALYSIS HUT

*"Check your anxieties at the door and throw away the claim tag."*

**LOVED ONES' EATING HABITS DRIVING YOU GA-GA? BOSS'S LUNKHEADEDNESS MAKING YOU TENSE AND IRRITABLE? SELF-ESTEEM-O-METER ON EMPTY?**

We guarantee you'll feel blissfully superior for at least 30 minutes, or your money back!

---

Try Dr. Monroe's special $79.95 workshops *du jour:*

**MONDAY:**
Guilt, Schmilt! Giving Your Superego the Old Head Fake

**TUESDAY:**
The Primal Scream: Keep That Racket Down, Willya?!

**WEDNESDAY:**
It's Not Your Fault: Shifting Blame the E-Z Way.

**THURSDAY:** Choosing the Right Preschool for Your Inner Child

**FRIDAY:**
Creative Denial: Hey, Forget It!

**WEEKENDS:** Dr. Monroe's Tough Love Retreat: Learn how to dish it out AND take it. (All family members must sign liability waiver.)

**INSOMNIACS!**
Try our 24-HOUR HOTLINE!
Soothing recorded counselors available around the clock!
**1-900-QUIKFIX**
95¢ per minute.
Touchtone phone required.

Opening Soon! Dr. Monroe's
## PSYCHO-PSNACK PSHOP!
Featuring...
• Prozac Shakes • Lithium Chip Cookies • Thorazine-On-A-Stick

---

## IN A HURRY?
When that panic attack just won't wait, tune up your neuroses for just $19.95 at the...

# MONROE-TO-GO
### JIFFY-KWIK 5-MINUTE DRIVE-THRU INTERACTIVE CENTERING AND FOCUSING WINDOW

**Three caring and understanding lanes to choose from:**
• Live Counselor (stuffed animal and kleenex optional)
• Video Counselor with remote control question-and-answer menu
• Speakerphone with counselor on audio cassette
(4-wheel drive vehicles add $5. Sorry, no big rigs or buses)

---

Looking for the perfect gift? Visit our
# NOVELTY NOOK
Featuring officially licensed DR. MARVIN MONROE products...
"His" and "Hers" Foam Rubber Mallets • Rose-Colored Glasses • Easy-to-Assemble Isolation Tanks
AND FOR THE KIDS: Itchy and Scratchy's "My Very Own Nightmare" Journal

---

## NUCLEAR POWER PLANT EMPLOYEES!

Don't miss Dr. Monroe's hit video cassette,
**"Feeling Good About Your Radiation Level"**
# 20% OFF
# WITH THIS COUPON
(Valid weekdays only, 9 to 5. Must show proof of 10 years' minimum exposure. Blood sample may be required.)

---

## YES! We have INTERACTIVE FAMILY ELECTROSHOCK THERAPY!

# SMILIN' JOE FISSION'S Fun Corner

UP 'N' ATOM, BOYS 'N' GIRLS!

YOU KNOW HOW YOU HATE TO TAKE OUT THE GARBAGE NO MATTER HOW MUCH YOUR MOM NAGS YOU... WELL, HEH, HEH! WE GROWN-UPS ARE KINDA THE SAME WAY ABOUT GETTING RID OF OUR NUCLEAR WASTE!

## CONSERVATION:
### PIE-IN-THE-SKY TOMFOOLERY OR DANGEROUS EXTREMISM?

In fact, it's both! Conservation is both impractical (after all, who wants less power?) and economically risky. Remember, the more power you use, the more we make! That means jobs for many of our citizens—maybe even your parents—and toys, clothes, and allowances for children like you!
So relax and enjoy, and leave the power to us!

### TODAY'S NUCLEAR BRAIN TEASER

Q: Where do you safely dispose of high-level liquid and solid radioactive waste?

A: If ANYONE has an answer to today's quiz, PLEASE contact the Nuclear Regulatory Commission as soon as possible!!

HEY, KIDS! GRAB A PENCIL AND SEE IF YOU CAN SOLVE TODAY'S ATOMIC BRAIN TWISTER!

HERE IN SPRINGFIELD THE MANY BLESSINGS OF NUCLEAR POWER ARE AVAILABLE TO ALL, NO MATTER HOW LOWLY THEIR SOCIAL STATUS. BUT DO YOU KNOW WHO THE BIGGEST BENEFICIARY IS? CONNECT THE DOTS AND FIND OUT!

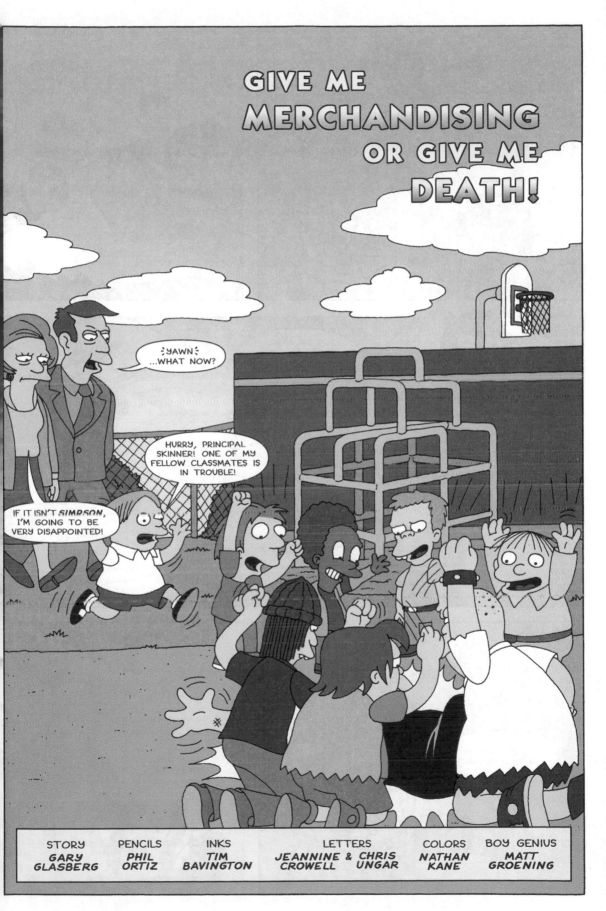

STORY
GARY
GLASBERG

PENCILS
PHIL
ORTIZ

INKS
TIM
BAVINGTON

LETTERS
JEANNINE & CHRIS
CROWELL    UNGAR

COLORS
NATHAN
KANE

BOY GENIUS
MATT
GROENING

ALL RIGHT... BREAK IT UP, EVERYBODY! SHOW'S OVER.

DO I LOOK LIKE *DON KING* TO YOU?!

HAD ENOUGH, THIEF?!

GIVE BACK WHAT YOU *STOLE*, LOWLIFE! IT'S OURS!

OUR INSURANCE POLICY DOESN'T COVER RECONSTRUCTIVE SURGERY! I SUGGEST YOU CALL YOUR PARENTS AND...

*GASP!!*

GROUNDSKEEPER WILLIE!!

ACH! IT'S ABOUT TIME, SKINNER! ANOTHER MINUTE AND ME *NOGGIN* WOULDA BEEN *SPLATTERED* ALL OVER THE TEETER-TOTTER!

OH, WILLIE! ARE YOU *HURT*? CAN YOU SEE ME?!

AYE, LASSIE! YE GOT MORE *CHIN HAIRS* THAN ME *GREAT UNCLE SHEAMUS!*

WHAT'S THIS ALL ABOUT?!

HE *STOLE* OUR *COMIC BOOK!*

GRABBED IT RIGHT OUTA MY HANDS!

I GOT CAUGHT UP IN THE HEAT OF *PASSION!* I THOUGHT I WAS IN *GYM CLASS!*

FOR HEAVEN'S SAKE, WILLIE, GIVE IT BACK! IT'S NOTHING BUT A STUPID COMIC BOOK!

DO YA REALIZE WHAT YER ASKIN', WOMAN? THIS IS THE LAST COPY OF *THE OYSTERIZER* ANYWHERE IN TOWN!

THE *WHAT?!*

*THE OYSTERIZER,* MA'AM. THE *GREATEST* UNDERGROUND COMIC TO HIT SPRINGFIELD ELEMEN-TARY IN *DECADES!!*

HEY!

AND WHO'S *RESPON-SIBLE* FOR THIS PHOTOCOPIED *WASTE* OF *WOOD PULP?!*

THAT NIGHT...

D'OH! DARN *BATTERIES*! I COULD'VE SWORN I JUST CHANGED THESE LAST WEEK!

HURRY, HOMEY! SWITCH THE CHANNEL. OUR FAVORITE CONSUMER INVESTIGATOR IS ABOUT TO UNCOVER ANOTHER SPRINGFIELD BUSINESS SCAM!!

GOOD EVENING, FOLKS. I'M *DAVE SHUTTON*. ON TONIGHT'S *"EYE FOR AN EYE"* WE RAISE THE QUESTION "ARE THE ALUMINUM FOIL SWAN-SHAPED DOGGIE BAGS USED BY RITZY EATERIES A WASTE OF PRECIOUS RESOURCES?" STAY TUNED!!

MMM, DOGGIE BAGS!

AND WHERE DO YOU THINK *YOU'RE* GOING, BART?

OOPS!

UM...WELL... MILHOUSE AND I WERE PLANNING ON GOING TO THE BIG SPRINGFIELD *COMIC CONVENTION*. REMEMBER?

YOU'VE BEEN *SUSPENDED*, YOUNG MAN. YOU'RE NOT GOING ANYWHERE!

BUT YOU CAN'T *GROUND* ME! NOT *NOW*! THE COMIC CONVENTION IS THE MOST *IMPORTANT DAY* OF THE YEAR! IF WE DON'T PRESENT *THE OYSTERIZER* AT TONIGHT'S PORTFOLIO REVIEW, WE'RE *FINISHED*!

CRUNCH!
CRUNCH!

NOW, WHAT'S SO *GREAT* ABOUT A BUNCH OF MAKE-BELIEVE *SUPERHEROES*, ANYWAY?! YOUR *FATHER* IS THE BEST *HERO* A BOY COULD HAVE!

MMM, POPCORN GREASE!

BUURP!!

YOU BROKE *SCHOOL RULES*, BART SIMPSON! NOW GO TO YOUR *ROOM* AND DON'T COME OUT UNTIL THE CONVENTION'S OVER!

⋵SIGH⋵ YES, MA'AM.

I GUESS SHE'S RIGHT. I MEAN, WHOEVER HEARD OF A GUY BECOMING A *MILLIONAIRE* BECAUSE HE CREATED A SILLY *CARTOON CHARACTER*, ANYWAY?!

LATER...

MAN, LOOK AT THE TIME! THE CONVENTION *CLOSES* IN TWO HOURS! WHAT AM I GONNA DO?!

YOUR *MA* DOESN'T KNOW NOTHIN', SQUIRT! THIS IS THE *CHANCE* OF A *LIFETIME!* BIG BUCKS! LIMOUSINES! *MILLIONS* OF KIDS *BEGGIN'* FOR YOUR *AUTOGRAPH!* YOU *GOTTA* BREAK OUTA THIS JOINT!!

*POOF!*

DON'T *LISTEN* TO HIM, BART! MOTHER KNOWS BEST! FAME AND FORTUNE QUICKLY CORRUPT! THERE'S MORE TO LIFE THAN VIDEO GAMES AND--

*POOF!*

GET *LOST,* HALO-HEAD! THE *DEVIL'S* RIGHT! THERE'S ONLY ONE THING LEFT TO DO!!

BARTRON TO MILBOT...BARTRON TO *MILBOT!!* COME IN!

WHAT'S UP, BARTRON?

MEET ME AT THE *CONVENTION CENTER,* MILBOT. IT'S NOW OR NEVER!!

REMEMBER, IF THEY OFFER US A *CONTRACT*, STAY COOL! YOU DON'T WANT TO SEEM NERVOUS!

WHAT IF I THROW UP?!

BOFFO COMICS

PORTFOLIO REVIEW

I'M LENNY... THIS IS JOEL. TO YOU, WE'RE GODS. YOU'VE GOT *THIRTY-FIVE SECONDS* TO ENTERTAIN US. JOEL HASN'T SMILED IN EIGHTEEN YEARS. *GO!*

CLICK

LENNY HUFFS

JOEL BINX

CHECK IT OUT! WHEN MASTER SCUBA INSTRUCTOR *DIRK DAWSON'S* DEPTH GAUGE FAILS, HE LOSES CONSCIOUSNESS AND SINKS TO THE BOTTOM OF THE SEA.

PLUMMETING INTO THE DARKNESS, HE LANDS DANGEROUSLY CLOSE TO A SHIPWRECKED *NUCLEAR SUBMARINE* AND BECOMES TRAPPED INSIDE THE SHELL OF A NEARBY GIANT OYSTER!

MONTHS LATER, HAVING GONE THROUGH AN *ATOMICALLY* ENHANCED META-MORPHOSIS, THE OYSTER OPENS, GIVING BIRTH TO THE WORLD'S LATEST AND GREATEST MUTANT SUPERHERO... *THE OYSTERIZER!*

YOUR *STORYLINES* ARE SIMPLISTIC...YOUR *LAYOUT'S* POORLY CONCEIVED.

LENNY HUFFS

BOFFO COMICS

JOEL BINX

SO, WHAT ARE YOU TRYING TO SAY?!

WELL?

I'VE SEEN MORE *INTERESTING* ARTWORK IN PUBLIC RESTROOMS!

LENNY HUFFS

JOEL

PERHAPS I CAN INTEREST YOU TWO FEEBLE-MINDED *TODDLERS* IN SOMETHING OTHER THAN BRAIN PABULUM! THIS IS THE NEW *MASTERPIECE* FROM BOFFO! I CAN'T UNPACK THE PULITZER PRIZE WINNER FAST ENOUGH! HOW MANY CAN I PUT YOU DOWN FOR?!

THANKS, BUT I'VE AL-READY GOT ONE AT HOME!

WHAT ARE WE GOING TO DO, BART?!

FROZEN PEARL OYSTER SNACKS

WE'RE PAY-ING A VISIT TO *BOFFO COMICS*, MILHOUSE! ARNOLD LEACH *OWES* US BIG TIME!!

FROZEN

LATER...

BOFFO A DIVISION OF BURNS INDUSTRIES

UH-OH!! I THINK THE *GUARD'S* ON-TO US!

WOULD YOU LIKE FRIES WITH THAT BURGER, YOUNG LADY?!

NO PROBLEMO!

**1 BILLION COPIES SOLD!**

BART, I DON'T THINK ANYBODY'S GOING TO *BELIEVE* US.

ARE YOU KIDDING?! I BET LENNY AND JOEL CAN'T WAIT TO SAY THANKS!

TO ARNOLD, THE PEARL

THE PEARL TRADING CARDS

CAN I HELP YOU?

TELL LEACH HIS *BOY GENIUSES* ARE HERE!!

I'M SORRY, BUT MR. LEACH IS ENTERTAINING GUESTS ON *THE PEARL* YACHT. IT'S A PARTY FOR THE COMIC'S CREATORS, LENNY AND JOEL.

THE COMIC'S CREATORS?! *AYE, CARUMBA!!*

THERE THEY ARE... *GET 'EM!!*

WHOOOOA!

TELL LEACH HE'LL BE HEARING FROM MY *MOUTHPIECE!!*

LATER...

IT'S LIKE THIS, HUTZ. MILHOUSE AND I THOUGHT UP *THE PEARL*, DREW *THE PEARL*, AND SHOWED *THE PEARL* TO BOFFO A FEW MONTHS AGO! NOW THEY'RE *RICH* AND WE'RE NOT!

DARN CUBE!! IT'S BEEN *TEASING* MY BRAIN FOR TWENTY YEARS. MAKE IT STOP!!

WE *DEMAND* JUSTICE AND COMPENSATION! A LITTLE RECOGNITION! OUR PIECE OF THE MEGA-MOOLA PIE!!

HEY, WATCH THE OAK FORMICA!

THUD!

SPRINGFIELD GAZZETTE

PEARL SETS WALL STREET A-WHIRL

LET ME GET THIS STRAIGHT. YOU EXPECT ME TO *BELIEVE* THAT YOU TWO LITTLE *PIP-SQUEAKS* CREATED THE BIGGEST SUPERHERO IN THE HISTORY OF ENTERTAINMENT MERCHANDISING?!

YESSIR!

I *REFUSE* TO TURN THIS OFFICE INTO A DEN OF *LIE TELLIN' GUYS* AND *DECEIT-MONGERS*! NOW, *GET OUT!!*

PSSST! KID! MEET ME IN THE ALLEY. WE NEED TO TALK *BUSINESS!*

½ OFF!

HUH?!

ALL RIGHT, WHAT'S THIS ALL ABOUT?!

THE DROID'S DUNGEON COMIC SHOP

POST NO BILLS

THE PEARL

HIYA, BOYS! RE-MEMBER ME? I WORK FOR BOFFO COMICS.

YOU'RE LENNY! YOU *STOLE* OUR IDEA!

I KNOW I'M A BUM, BUT A CHARACTER LIKE *THE PEARL* DOESN'T COME ALONG VERY OFTEN!

YOU GUYS CREATED SOME-THIN' WORTH *MILLIONS* AND NOW *THE PEARL* NEEDS YOUR HELP!!

WHAT *KIND* OF HELP?!

YOU TWO COME TO *WORK* AT BOFFO AND SAVE *THE PEARL* FROM FI-NANCIAL FAILURE!

AND WHAT DO WE GET IN RETURN?!

CONTRACT
I, BART SIMPSON

CONTRACT
I, MILHOUSE VAN HOUTEN

MONTGOMERY BURNS OWNS BOFFO COMICS. YOU GUYS SAY NO, LEACH PULLS SOME STRINGS, AND BART'S OLD MAN IS *OUT OF A JOB!* UNDERSTOOD?!

THE PEARL

THAT'S *BLACKMAIL!*

THAT'S *BUSINESS!* TAKE IT OR LEAVE IT! WHAT'S IT GONNA BE?!

SIGN IT, DUDE. I'VE GOT AN IDEA!!

LATER...

YOU MEAN, THAT CRUMMY COMIC BOOK YOU USED TO WORK ON IS ACTUALLY *THE PEARL?!*

BART, THIS TIME EVEN I'M IMPRESSED!!

I KNOW IT'S HARD TO BELIEVE, SIS, BUT IT'S TRUE. BOFFO STOLE IT FROM RIGHT UNDER OUR NOSES!

NOW THEY'RE *BLACKMAILING* US INTO WORKING FOR THEM OR THEY'LL HAVE MR. BURNS *FIRE* DAD!!

THAT'S WHERE *YOU* COME IN, LISA!

SINCE YOU CAN'T GO *PUBLIC* YOURSELF, YOU HAVE NO CHOICE BUT TO PLANT A *SECRET MESSAGE* IN AN UPCOMING ISSUE ACCUSING LEACH OF *PLAGIARISM* AND *SLIMY BUSINESS PRACTICES!* BUT HOW?!

I HAVE AN IDEA!!

A FEW DAYS LATER...

GOOD MORNING, CONSUMER RESEARCHERS! ANYTHING *JUICY* IN TODAY'S MAILBAG?!

EYE FOR AN EYE

WEEKNITES CHANNEL8

EYE FOR AN EYE

WELL, MR. SHUTTON, I HAVE A COMPANY THAT CLAIMS ITS HIGH PRICED TOASTER WILL BURN THE IMAGE OF A RELIGIOUS LEADER INTO AN ENGLISH MUFFIN!!

NICE TRY, SON. BUT GIVE YOUR UNCLE DAVE SOMETHING HE CAN SINK HIS TEETH INTO!

MEANWHILE...

BART, WE HAVEN'T *SLEPT* IN DAYS! I CAN'T KEEP THIS UP MUCH LONGER!

HOLD ON, MILHOUSE! JUST A FEW MORE DRAWINGS!

THAT'S THE *SPIRIT*, SIMPSON! JUST A FEW MORE DRAWINGS. AND THEN A FEW *HUNDRED* MORE AFTER THAT!

BOSS

THANKS TO THAT *PARENTAL RELEASE* BURNS CONNED YOUR FATHER INTO SIGNING, *YOU'RE MINE!!*

SALES ARE RIGHT BACK ON TRACK, BUDDY!

WE COULDN'T HAVE DONE IT WITHOUT YOU, BART! IF YOU KNOW WHAT I MEAN?

KEEP UP THE GOOD WORK, VAN HOUTEN! IF YOU'RE NICE, I'LL PAY YOU IN BACK ISSUES!!

HA-HA!

COFF!

ARNOLD LEACH... DAVE SHUTTON, *EYE FOR AN EYE!* IS IT *TRUE* YOU *STOLE* THE IDEA FOR *THE PEARL?* WHO'S THE *RIGHTFUL HEIR* TO THE PEARL FORTUNE?!

CRASH!

WHO THE...?

WOO-HOO! GO GET HIM, DAVE!!

SHUT UP, YOU IDIOT!

*IT'S A LIE!* I CAME UP WITH THE *CLAM GUY* MYSELF!

I WAS WOLFIN' DOWN SOME FISH STICKS WHEN IT CAME TO ME IN A DREAM! SO, SOME *KID* AT A CONVENTION HAD THE IDEA FIRST... PROVE IT!!

WE DID IT, MILHOUSE!!

WEEKS LATER...

SIMPSON, I'M TEMPORARILY SENDING YOU TO WORK FOR MY *COMIC BOOK COMPANY*.

DON'T ASK ANY QUESTIONS! JUST DO AS YOUR TOLD BY YOUR NEW *SUPERVISOR!!*

MONTGOMERY BURNS

BUT, SIR...

GO!!!

WHY DO I HAVE TO GO WORK AT A DUMB COMIC BOOK FACTORY, ANYWAY?!

SIR, IT'S HOMER SIMPSON. MAY I COME IN?

SUITE 201

*Boffo! BOSS*

MY BOSS IS PROBABLY SOME NASTY OLD STICK IN THE MUD!!

THAT AFTERNOON...

MR. BURNS AND I STRUCK A *DEAL!* HE DOESN'T GET *PROSECUTED* AND I GET A COOL *SUMMER JOB* COMPLETE WITH A BALDING YET SOMEHOW LOVABLE ASSISTANT! PRETTY AWESOME, HUH?!

BART, YOU'RE THE BEST SON...UM BOSS...A MAN COULD EVER HAVE!!

*Boffo! BOSS*

BOY?!

HOMER!!

BART SIMPSON

THAT'S *"MR. BART"* TO YOU!!

D'OH!

THE END

# REBEL WITHOUT A CLUTCH

WHOA, DUDES! CHECK OUT THAT *DIRTBIKE!*

WISH I HAD A SET OF *WHEELS* LIKE THAT!

YEAH! IF I HAD A DIRTBIKE, I'D BE AS *TOUGH* AS THAT *JAY LENO* DUDE!

| BARRY DUTTER | SHAUN CASHMAN | CHRIS UNGAR | NATHAN KANE | MATT GROENING |
|---|---|---|---|---|
| STORY | ART | LETTERS | COLORS | HOOLIGAN |

YOU CAN FORGET THOSE *TAILPIPE DREAMS* OF YOURS, BOYS!

THIS DIRTBIKE IS THE *PRIZE* IN *SPRINGFIELD ELEMENTARY'S* ANNUAL ART FESTIVAL & BAKE OFF!

THE ONLY WAY YOU'LL BE RIDING *THIS* BABY IS IF YOU THREE *HOODLUMS* SUDDENLY LEARN HOW TO *EXPRESS* YOURSELVES *CREATIVELY!*

NOW, WHY DON'T YOU RUN ALONG! AND DON'T LET ME *CATCH* YOU GIVING ANY OF YOUR *INVOLUNTARY MUDBATHS!*

THOSE PUNKS ARE A *WASTE* OF TIME! THEY'LL NEVER *LEARN* ANYTHING!

SAY, THAT *REMINDS* ME -- EXACTLY WHY IS A *DIRTBIKE* BEING GIVEN AWAY AS A PRIZE IN AN *ARTS & CRAFTS SHOW?*

WE WANTED *ALL* THE KIDS TO ENTER, NOT JUST THE *ART NERDS!*

MAYBE THERE'S A WAY YOU *CAN* GET *BACK* AT HIM, *JIMBO!*

THAT LOUSY *SKINNER!* I'D LIKE TO *SKIN* HIM!

YOU MEAN *KIDNAP* HIS *MOM* AGAIN?

NO -- SOMETHING EVEN *BETTER!*

YOU COULD *STEAL* THAT DIRTBIKE!

YEAH -- THAT WOULD *REALLY* STICK IT TO *THE MAN,* MAN!

YOU'RE *RIGHT!* I'LL *DO* IT!

CAN YOU *HOT-WIRE* THAT BIKE, *JIMBO?*

I *THINK* SO!

BUT I NEED YOU GUYS TO MAKE SOME KIND OF, UM, LIKE, *DISTRACTION!*

YOU *GOT* IT! IF THERE ARE KIDS WITH *PANTS* NEARBY, WE'RE JUST THE GUYS WHO CAN PULL'EM *DOWN!*

SOON...

I WAS *BORN* TO BE *WILD,* AN' I'M *BAD* TO THE *BONE!*

VRRROOOM!

GO, *JIMBO!*

AFTER MONTHS OF *PAINSTAKING* WORK, IT'S *FINISHED!* MY HAND-CRAFTED MODEL OF THE *STARSHIP* FROM L. RON HUBBARD'S *BATTLEFIELD: EARTH* -- MADE ENTIRELY FROM *TOOTHPICKS!*

PERHAPS THIS DISPLAY OF MY *ARTISTIC PROWESS* WILL FINALLY WIN ME THE RESPECT OF MY *FELLOW CLASSMATES!*

LOOK OUT! MY *MODEL!*

THE ONLY THING *COOLER* THAN *CUTTIN' SCHOOL* -- IS CUTTIN' SCHOOL ON A *DIRTBIKE!*

BOINK!

WHOA! A *UFO!*

OKAY, THAT'S TWO SCRUMPTIOUS *KRUSTY BURGERS*, ONE ORDER OF *DELICIOUS FRIES*, THREE TASTY *CLOWNION RINGS*, ONE SUCCULENT *APPLE CREAM PIE...*

*PATIENCE*, STOMACH! SOON, THIS WILL *ALL* BE YOURS...!

THERE'D BETTER BE SOME *EXTRA KETCHUP* IN HERE!

YAAGH!

MY PRECIOUS *FAST FOOD* -- LADEN WITH ESSENTIAL *GREASE* AND *SALT!*

IT'S ALL *GONE!*

COME BACK AND PAY FOR THAT *CHERRY SQUISHEE*, YOU YOUNG *RUFFIAN!*

AW, YOUR MOTHER WEARS.. UH...UM...I DUNNO... A *HAT*, I GUESS!

CALLING ALL UNITS!

WE HAVE A REPORT OF A *TEEN-AGER* ON A *DIRT-BIKING RAMPAGE OF DESTRUCTION* AND *PETTY LARCENY!*

THAT'S NOT *MY* PROBLEM!

WHAT THE --?!

YOU'VE HAD ENOUGH DONUTS FOR ONE DAY, *FATSO!*

YOINK!

*BIG MISTAKE*, KID! YOU JUST MADE IT *PERSONAL!*

IN THE KITCHEN...

MARGE, WE'RE HOME. IS DINNER READY?

JUST ABOUT.

HOMEY, THAT'S NOT GRAMPA!

THIS IS SAM.

HOMER, THIS WAS SUPPOSED TO BE A FAMILY DINNER.

BUT, MARGE, THEY'RE BOTH OLD! WHAT'S THE DIFFERENCE?

≡MOAN≡

SOMETHING SURE SMELLS GOOD.

IT SURE ISN'T SAM.

THIS MUST BE HIS FIRST MEAL IN WEEKS. KIDS, WHAT YOUR FATHER DID WAS...UM...IMPULSIVE, BUT STILL VERY NOBLE.

YEAH, DAD SHOULD BE COMMENDED. HE HEARD THE DESPERATE PLEAS OF THE DISEN- FRANCHISED AND SAID...

SHOVEL! SNARF! SHOVEL!

MMM, GRISTLE!

AFTER DINNER...

IN *MY* FAMILY, WE USED TO SPEND EVENINGS CREATING OUR *OWN* ENTERTAINMENT. WE WOULD SHARE ALL OF OUR SPECIAL TALENTS AND ABILITIES BECAUSE WE HAD NO *TELEVISION*.

WE WOULD PERFORM MAGIC TRICKS...

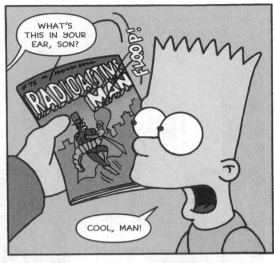

WHAT'S THIS IN YOUR EAR, SON?

FLOOP!

RADIOACTIVE MAN

COOL, MAN!

...SING SONGS, JUGGLE, YOU NAME IT!

LATER...

MARGE, THANK YOU FOR A LOVELY EVENING. IT TAKES A CERTAIN KIND OF COMPASSION AND DISREGARD FOR ONE'S PERSONAL SAFETY TO LET A TOTAL STRANGER INTO THEIR HOME.

I WILL NOT FORGET YOUR HUSBAND'S ACT OF KINDNESS.

GOOD-BYE, SAM.

BUT, SAM, WHERE WILL YOU *GO*?

DON'T WORRY ABOUT ME, I'LL BE JUST FINE.

WHOOOSH!

WHOA, MAMA!

THE NEXT MORNING...

MR. SIMPSON!
*MR. SIMPSON!*

SKRITCH
SKRITCH

*SLAM*

MORNIN', HOMER. WANNA WATCH THAT MASTERFUL, RIB-TICKLING, SATIRIST KNOWN AS *KRUSTY THE KLOWN*?

≡MUMBLE≡

*HEY!* THEY'RE INTERRUPTING THE *CLOWNIEST CLOWN* ON EARTH FOR SOME LOUSY *GROWN-UP* STORY.

*Special Report*

BE *QUIET*, BART. *SPECIAL REPORTS* HERALD MONUMENTAL OCCASIONS IN ONE'S LIFE. IT COULD BE AN ANNOUNCEMENT OF A PRECEDENT-SETTING CHANGE IN FOREIGN POLICY, THE DISCOVERY OF A CURE FOR A PREVIOUSLY INCURABLE DISEASE, OR...

WE INTERRUPT THIS PROGRAM, QUITE FRANKLY...

HEH, HEH

BECAUSE WE *CAN*!

...A FLAGRANT DISPLAY OF THE NEWS MEDIA'S TOTALITARIAN GRIP ON THE AIRWAVES.

IT SEEMS THAT SPRINGFIELD'S *NEWEST* BILLIONAIRE IS AS RECLUSIVE AS HIS BENE-FACTOR. HE *REFUSES* TO BE INTERVIEWED AND SCURRIED BACK INSIDE WHEN FIRST ENCOUNTERING THE MEDIA MOB OUTSIDE HIS...MANSION.

HEH-HEH. ALLITERATION, A NEWSMAN'S POETRY.

RECORDED EARLIER

HOMER, DO YOU SEE WHAT *I* SEE?

YEAH, SO? IT'S JUST SOME NEWS GUY TALKING ABOUT SOMEBODY BEING PUT INTO THAT OLD GUY'S WILL, WHILE AT THE SAME TIME THEY'RE SHOWING A VIDEOTAPE OF *ME* GETTING THE MORNING PAPER.

IT'S NOT LIKE THEY SAID *I* INHERITED A WHOLE *BEER EMPIRE* AND *BILLIONS OF DOLLARS*, NOW IS IT, MRS. SMARTY-PANTS?

SO FAR, LITTLE IS KNOWN ABOUT THE NEW OWNER OF THE DUFF BREWERIES OTHER THAN HIS NAME, *HOMER J. SIMPSON!*

D'OH!

I'M SORRY ABOUT THE SMARTY-PANTS THING, MARGE. I WAS WRONG.

I'M A *BILLIONAAAAIRE!*
I'M A *BILLIONAAAAIRE!*
I'M A *BILLIONAAAAIRE!*

WELL, WHAM-BAM, THANK YOU, *SAM!*

MEANWHILE...

SMITHERS!

HERE IT IS, SIR. YOUR OTHER CONTACT LENS.

AHH! ONCE AGAIN IN THE LAND OF DEPTH PERCEPTION!

LOOK AT THIS CHICANERY, SMITHERS. A WORKING STIFF TAKES IN A HAPLESS HOBO, GIVES HIM A QUAINT, SUBURBAN SUPPER AND THE NEXT DAY HE'S BEQUEATHED A BILLION DOLLAR BEER FORTUNE.

ONLY IN AMERICA, SIR.

HMMM, MAKES YOU WONDER IF THAT'S WHAT THE FOUNDING FATHERS REALLY HAD IN MIND WHEN THEY CAME UP WITH THAT WHOLE "FREEDOM" CONCEPT.

WHO IS THIS HOMER SIMPSON?

HE'S ONE OF OUR SAFETY INSPECTORS.

WELL, HE'S FIRED! NOW LET'S SEE HIM TRY TO LIVE ON A MEASLY BILLION DOLLARS!

SO, THIS DO-GOODER THINKS HE CAN RUN A BREWERY. WELL, AS MUCH AS I ENJOY WATCHING MONEY AND POWER CORRUPT A MAN'S SOUL, I'LL NEVER BE ONE-UPPED BY SOME HOMER-COME-LATELY!

SMITHERS, I HAVE A PLAN.

THE NEXT DAY...

IS EVERYONE READY FOR THE V.I.P. TOUR?

YEAH, YEAH, YEAH! DO I GET *FREE BEER?*

WOO HOO!

HA, HA. OF COURSE YOU DO, MR. SIMPSON. AFTER ALL, IT'S *YOUR* BREWERY NOW.

BART, WHY DO I HAVE A VISION OF BEING ON A TALK SHOW DESCRIBING THIS VERY MOMENT AS THE LOW POINT OF MY CHILDHOOD?

C'MON, LISA. DEEP DOWN YOU CAN SMELL A MONEY MAKING-OPPORTUNITY AS WELL AS *I* CAN.

≈MOAN≈

BEHIND THIS FOUNTAIN LIES THE SOURCE OF OUR BEER'S DISTINCTIVE TASTE--THE *CRYSTAL CLEAR* WATERS OF *DUFF SPRINGS!*

SINCE 1973, WHEN SKYROCKETING COSTS FORCED US OFF THE MUNICIPAL WATER SUPPLY, DUFF BEER HAS COME TO YOU *STRAIGHT FROM NATURE.*

NO TRESPASS PROPERTY OF *Duff* ENTERPRISES

NO SWIMMING, WADI FISHING OR--WATER

CLOSED BY ORDER OF PRES. TRUMAN

QUARANTINED

SPRINGFIELD PLANT

LATER...

HERE'S WHERE DUFF BEER IS PROPERLY AGED TO ACHIEVE ITS FINE, SMOOTH CHARACTER. TAKE A TASTE, MR. SIMPSON.

Duff
Duff LITE
Duff DRY

MMM... CHARACTER!

WHOA, THERE, MR. SIMPSON! WE'D BETTER LEAVE SOME FOR OUR PAYING CUSTOMERS.

HUH? OH, YEAH. HEE-HEE.

ANY QUESTIONS, MR. SIMPSON?

LET'S SEE... I CAN WORK WHENEVER I WANT, DRINK A LOT OF FREE BEER, UM...

WHEN DO WE MEET THE NORWEGIAN G-STRING GIRLS?

A SIX-PACK OF SHAME.

MR. SIMPSON, THOSE GALS AREN'T REALLY FROM NORWAY. THEY'RE JUST THREE SCANTILY CLAD WOMEN FROM OUR MARKETING DEPARTMENT. BUT, THEY SURE DO SELL THE DUFF!

THIS IS IT, MR. SIMPSON, THE MOMENT YOU HAVE BEEN WAITING FOR.

CHUGFEST?

NO. THE BOARD OF DIRECTORS IS READY TO SEE YOU.

MR. BURNS! WHAT ARE *YOU* DOING HERE?

*SURPRISE,* SIMPSON. MEET THE PROUD OWNER OF *FORTY-NINE PERCENT* OF DUFF INDUSTRIES.

WHO?

ME, YOU IDIOT!

OH. WAIT A MINUTE... LET'S SEE, FORTY-NINE PERCENT...OUT OF ONE HUNDRED PERCENT... CARRY THE ONE...

MARGE, IF HE OWNS FORTY-NINE PER...

YOU OWN *FIFTY-ONE* PERCENT.

D'OH!

I *KNEW* IT WAS TOO GOOD TO BE TRUE.

WAP!

DAD, *YOU* OWN MORE.

WOO HOO!

I OWN *MORE!* I OWN *MORE!*

I WOULDN'T BREAK OUT THE CHAMPALE JUST YET.

*YOU* MAY BE SAM'S CHOSEN HEIR, BUT AS EXECUTOR OF THE WILL AND THE ONLY DUFF OFFICER ALIVE AND UNSCATHED BY THE *SYRINGE-IN-THE-BOTTLE* INCIDENT, I MUST DECIDE IF YOU ARE *TRULY WORTHY* OF HIS FORTUNE.

NO FAIR! YOU *KNOW* ME!

YES. I KNOW YOU AND I'VE DEVISED SOME SIMPLE, YET PRACTICALLY *INSURMOUNTABLE* TESTS FOR YOU.

TESTS?

SOON...

NOW, MR. SIMPSON, ALL YOU HAVE TO DO IS TAKE A LITTLE NAP.

A NAP, HUH? *NOBODY* NAPS LIKE *HOMER!*

YES, OFF TO *DREAMLAND*, SIMPSON.

A BRILLIANT IDEA, SIR. HE'LL NEVER FEEL THAT BEER NUT UNDERNEATH ALL THOSE CUSHIONS.

CAN'T... GET... COMFY...

FIDGET!

STRUGGLE!

SPROING!

AAAGH! LOOK OUT!

MMM... *BEER NUT!*

UNBELIEVABLE! HE PASSED THE TEST!

DAMN HIM AND HIS *SEN-SITIVE BUTT!*

BONK!

113

A FEW TESTS LATER...

NOW, FOR YOUR FINAL CHALLENGE, A SIMPLE *TASTE TEST*.

CORRECTLY IDENTIFY THE DIFFERENT TYPES OF DUFF BEER FROM THE SELECTION WITHIN, AND THE FORTUNE IS YOURS!

TODAY, I CONSIDER MYSELF THE LUCKIEST MAN ON EARTH!

DUFF RED!

DUFF ICE!

DUFF... SSSPECIAL RESSSERVE!

HERE YOU GO, MR. SIMPSON, JUST ONE LAST BREW AND YOU WILL *HAVE* YOUR BLASTED EMPIRE.

A QUARTER DUFF DRAFT, AN EIGHTH DUFF DRY...AN EIGHTH DUFF MALT...AN EIGHTH DUFF LAGER...AN EIGHTH DUFF CHRISTMAS ALE...AND...AN EIGHTH, NO A QUARTER...DUFF AMBER FIRE-BREWED BARLEY EXPORT, WHICH IS ONLY SOLD...IN *CANADA!*

I'M AFRAID HE'S RIGHT, SIR.

BLAST HIS TASTE BUDS! I *MEAN* IT, SMITHERS. I WANT YOU TO FIND SOMEONE TO *BLAST* HIS *TASTEBUDS!*

114

THE NEXT MORNING...

HEY, DAD, GET OVER YOUR HANGOVER AND LOOK AT THESE REPORTS I FOUND IN SAM'S FILES.

I DON'T HAVE A HANGOVER, LISA, THIS IS THE WAY *ALL* EXECUTIVES WORK.

WELL, IF YOU CAN FIND TIME IN YOUR *BUSY* SCHEDULE, I THOUGHT YOU MIGHT FIND IT INTERESTING TO SEE RECENT REPORTS FROM THE BOARD OF DIRECTORS.

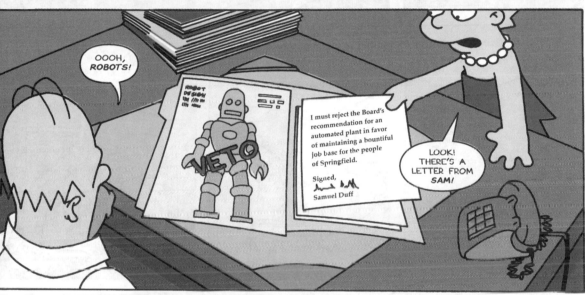

OOOH, *ROBOTS!*

ROBOT DESIGN

VETO

I must reject the Board's recommendation for an automated plant in favor of maintaining a bountiful job base for the people of Springfield.

Signed,
Samuel Duff

LOOK! THERE'S A LETTER FROM *SAM!*

MEANWHILE...

Duff    Duff

I'M NOT KIDDING YOU BOYS, MY OLD MAN CAN EAT *TWO-DOZEN JELLY DONUTS* IN ONE SITTING.

YOUR FATHER REALLY MUST HAVE A WORKING MAN'S DIGESTIVE TRACT.

SO, YOU FELLAS GOT ANY SUGGESTIONS FOR THE NEW MANAGEMENT TEAM?

BART, JUST KEEP EVERYTHING THE WAY MR. DUFF LEFT IT. I WOULDN'T CHANGE A THING.

IN THE CONFERENCE ROOM...

AS THE NEW OWNER OF DUFF BREWERY, I HAVE DECIDED TO MAKE A FEW ITSY-BITSY CHANGES. FIRST OF ALL, WE'LL BE INTRODUCING A NEW BEER.

GENTLEMEN, WHO AMONG US DOES NOT ENJOY STARTING OFF THE DAY WITH THAT MOST *DEE-LICIOUS* OF PASTRIES KNOWN AS *THE DONUT*?

AND, OF COURSE, WE *ALL* LOVE BEER.

SO, IN THE SPIRIT OF A CERTAIN PEANUT BUTTER CUP WE ALL KNOW AND LOVE, I WOULD LIKE TO INTRODUCE... *DUFF'S DOUBLE-DUNKIN' BREAKFAST LAGER!*

YOU MUST BE JOKING, YOU THREE-FINGERED *SLOTH!*

I *NEVER* JOKE ABOUT BEER. RIGHT, BARNEY?

*UURRP!*

D'OH!

SMITHERS, QUICKLY, WE MUST *DO* SOMETHING. SIMPSON IS DRIVING MY BREWERY INTO THE *GROUND!* WE'VE NO TIME TO LOSE.

WHERE DO YOU WANT THESE?

ROBOTS
PROPERTY OF *Salon Des Presidents EURO KRUSTY LAND*
ROBOTS

WE DIDN'T ORDER ANY *ROBOTS!*

OH, YES WE DID. *I* ORDERED THEM. I REVIEWED THE BOARD'S PLAN FOR AN AUTOMATED BREWERY AND OVERTURNED SAM'S VETO. HEH, HEH, US ROCK'N'FELLA TYPES GOT TO STICK TOGETHER, EH, BURNSY?

SMITHERS, I WILL NOT HAVE MY BREWERY OPERATED BY THAT LARD-BOTTOMED...

HEY!

~TAFT~ HE NEVER VETOED DESSERT

HE WAS TALKING ABOUT *TAFT.*

OH.

I WAS NEARLY *TARRED AND FEATHERED* FOR THINKING UP THAT AUTOMATION SCHEME. IF HE IMPLEMENTS IT, HE WILL BE THE MOST *REVILED* MAN IN SPRINGFIELD.

THOUGH IT PAINS ME TO *LOSE* THAT DISTINCTION, I AM HATCHING YET *ANOTHER* PLAN TO TAKE MY RIGHTFUL PLACE AS DUFF CHAIRMAN.

SMITHERS, HOW DO YOU FEEL ABOUT GOING *UNDERCOVER?*

I THOUGHT YOU'D NEVER ASK, SIR.

THE NEXT DAY...

WHY BOTHER COMING TO WORK IF I CAN BE REPLACED BY MILLARD FILLMORE?

YEAH. WHERE DOES SIMPSON GET OFF THINKING A *PRESIDENT* CAN PERFORM MINDLESS, REPETITIVE TASKS BETTER THAN *US*?

FIRST HE CREATES THAT DISGUSTING NEW DONUT BEER, NOW *THIS*! I NEVER THOUGHT I'D GROW TO HATE A CUSHY *UNION JOB*!

PERHAPS A *STRIKE* WOULD LET THE HIGHER-UPS KNOW HOW WE FEEL.

YEAH, *WE* COULD STOP WORKING, BUT HOW DO WE GET *THEM* TO STOP WORKING?

NO PROBLEM!

MY DEAR FRIENDS, I FEEL YOUR *SADNESS*. I KNOW YOUR *PAIN*. THIS ONCE GREAT BREWERY IS BEING RUN INTO THE GROUND. AND WHO DO WE HAVE TO THANK?

BOO!

HISS!

SIMPSON!

I THINK WE'D ALL BE BETTER OFF IF THE BREWERY WERE IN *MY* HANDS. *LET'S GO, BOYS!*

TO THE PICKET LINES, MY GOOD MEN!

WOO HOO!

YEAH!

AH, *SIMPSON*. I WANT TO HAVE A LITTLE EXCHANGE OF IDEAS... *YOUR* IDEAS WILL BE EXCHANGED BY *MINE*.

B-B-BUT... I STILL RUN THIS COMPANY. REMEMBER, *FIFTY-ONE* PERCENT.

*YAAAGH!*

WHAT GOOD IS CONTROL OF A FACTORY FULL OF DISENCHANTED *BOOZEHOUNDS*? TAKE A GOOD LOOK, SIMPSON. YOU'RE REIGN OF *ERROR* IS OVER.

NO ONE WILL BUY YOUR PRODUCTS, NO ONE WILL WORK IN YOUR FACTORY, AND YOUR PRES-IDENTIAL *FRIENDS* WILL BE DESTROYED.

BUT IT'S STILL *MY* BREWERY.

GOOD, GOOD! I'M GLAD TO SEE THERE'S STILL ENOUGH FIGHT IN YOU TO MAKE THIS AMUSING. GIVE IN SIMPSON! SELL ME YOUR SHARES AND MY TAKEOVER OF THE DUFF EMPIRE WILL BE *COMPLETE!*

AND IF I SAY *NO?*

AH, I SEE SAM HAS TAUGHT YOU *WELL.*

IT'S POINTLESS TO RESIST, SIMPSON. YOU *MUST* GIVE IN.

THE NEXT DAY...

THREE HUNDRED DOLLARS IS A LOT OF MONEY, HOMEY. WE CAN *STILL* CARPET THE BASEMENT.

IT'S NOT THE MONEY, MARGE. IT'S THAT I *FAILED*... *AGAIN!* AND AT SOMETHING AS SIMPLE AS RUNNING A BILLION DOLLAR BEER EMPIRE.

IT WASN'T A TOTAL LOSS, DAD. I LEARNED THAT MINDLESS AUTOMATONS WILL NOT MAKE HUMAN LABORERS OBSOLETE.

YEAH, AND I GOT TO EXPERIENCE THE LIFE OF A NE'ER-DO-WELL PLAYBOY SPONGING OFF THE FAMILY FORTUNE.

AND I GOT TO SEE THAT I LOVE MY HUSBAND, NO MATTER *WHERE* HE WORKS...OR DOESN'T. MAYBE MR. BURNS WILL GIVE YOU YOUR OLD JOB BACK.

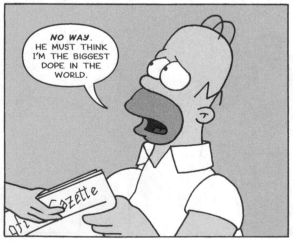

*NO WAY.* HE MUST THINK I'M THE BIGGEST DOPE IN THE WORLD.

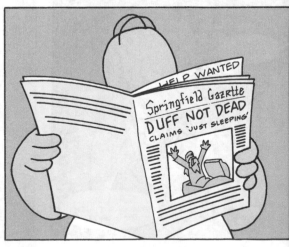

HELP WANTED

Springfield Gazette

DUFF NOT DEAD

CLAIMS 'JUST SLEEPING'

ELSEWHERE...

HOW CAN THIS BE? HE *DIED* OVER A *WEEK* AGO!

A RARE OCCURRENCE, SIR. I'M AS SURPRISED AS YOU ARE.

THIS MEANS THAT SIMPSON NEVER *LEGALLY* CONTROLLED DUFF! AND TO THINK, I GAVE HIM *THREE-HUNDRED DOLLARS!* THAT MAN IS SMARTER THAN HE LOOKS, SMITHERS. FIND OUT IF HE WOULD ACCEPT A POSITION AT THE NUCLEAR PLANT.

YOU *COULD* EMPLOY THE ROBOTS, SIR.

I RUN A *NUCLEAR POWER PLANT*, SMITHERS. I CAN'T LEAVE THE SAFETY OF MILLIONS IN THE HANDS OF *UNTHINKING MACHINES!* THIS TOWN DESERVES NO LESS THAN...WHAT WAS HIS NAME AGAIN?

SOON AFTER...

WELCOME BACK HOMER!

ZZZZZZZZ...

THE END

GRAMPA SIMPSON
AND HIS CRANKY PAL JASPER IN

# Nostalgia ain't what it used to be

| SCOTT SHAW! | TIM BAVINGTON | CHRIS UNGAR | NATHAN KANE | MATT GROENING |
|---|---|---|---|---|
| STORY & PENCILS | INKS | LETTERS | COLORS | PACKRAT |